STUDENT

VEGETARIAN

COOKBOOK

The Ultimate Guide to Easy and Delicious Vegetarian Cooking

LANE J. KIRK

Table of Contents

INTRODUCTION

Whether you're a longtime vegetarian or just getting started with a plant-based diet, cooking delicious vegetarian meals on a student budget can seem daunting. But never fear this Student Vegetarian Cookbook is here to help! As a student myself, I know firsthand the challenges of preparing affordable, nutritious meals in a dorm kitchen or shared apartment. Ramen noodles and frozen pizzas get old fast, and dining hall options can be hit-or-miss for vegetarians. That's why I've compiled this collection of vegetarian recipes specifically tailored for students. In this book, you'll find over 150 meatless recipes covering breakfast, lunch, dinner, and everything in between. From quick grab-and-go snacks to hearty main dishes, there's something for every craving and occasion. Best of all, the recipes all call for basic, inexpensive ingredients that any student can find at their local grocery store. Mornings just got easier with breakfast classics like overnight oats, tofu scrambles, and breakfast burritos. When the midday munchies strike, refuel with protein-packed salads, veggie-stuffed sandwiches, and crave-worthy appetizers like roasted chickpeas and zucchini fries. After a long day of classes, skip the overpriced (and unhealthy) take-out and instead whip up a satisfying veggie stir-fry, comforting bowl of chili, or pan of cheesy baked pasta. Along with entrees, you'll find plenty of flavorful sides like creamy mac and cheese, roasted Brussels sprouts, and mashed potatoes. This book is more than just a collection of meat-free recipes though. You'll also find tips for stocking your pantry on a budget, must-have kitchen equipment for small spaces, and easy meal prep tricks to save time and money. From my own experience, I know being a vegetarian student doesn't have to mean living off potato chips and cereal. With this cookbook as your guide, you can enjoy a wide variety of wholesome, delicious, and affordable vegetarian meals no matter your cooking skills or kitchen setup. Get ready to eat well without breaking the bank!

BRIEF OVERVIEW OF VEGETARIANISM FOR STUDENTS

Going vegetarian in college can seem daunting at first, but it's totally doable with the right knowledge and tools. As a vegetarian student myself, I know first-hand the challenges of cooking veggie meals on a budget with limited time and kitchen space. But I've learned that skipping meat doesn't have to mean skimping on flavor, nutrition or your social life. There are lots of great reasons why many students decide to go vegetarian: It's inexpensive. Cutting out meat products can make groceries way more affordable on a student budget. Plant-based staples like beans, lentils, pasta, rice and seasonal veggies give you the best bang for your buck. It's better for the environment. The meat industry leaves a hefty carbon footprint. Going veggie reduces your impact on things like fossil fuel consumption, greenhouse gas emissions and water usage. It's nutritious. When done right, a balanced vegetarian diet can be just as nutritious as any other diet. With smart meal planning, you'll get all the protein, iron, vitamins and nutrients you need to power through classes, activities and social events. It aligns with your values. For many, choosing a vegetarian lifestyle reflects a commitment to ethical treatment of animals or certain cultural/religious beliefs. As a student, it's empowering to stand up for the causes you care about.

There are different types of vegetarian diets to consider:

Locofoco vegetarians avoid meat, poultry and seafood, but do consume dairy products and eggs.

Lato vegetarians avoid meat, poultry, seafood and eggs, but do consume dairy products.

Ovo vegetarians avoid meat, poultry, seafood and dairy, but do consume eggs.

Vegans avoid all animal products including meat, poultry, seafood, eggs and dairy.

Plant-based diets consist mostly of plant foods like fruits, veggies, grains, legumes and nuts while minimizing animal products. The most common reasons students go vegetarian are health, environmental sustainability, ethical issues involving animals, or food allergies/intolerances. Religious or cultural traditions like Hinduism, Buddhism, Rastafarianism and Seventh Day Adventism also encourage plant-based eating. No matter your personal motivations, it's crucial to construct a balanced vegetarian diet that provides all the protein, vitamins and minerals your body needs, especially during the demanding college years. With this cookbook as your guide, you'll learn simple tips and tasty recipes to make vegetarian eating easy, nutritious and seriously delicious!

THE IMPORTANCE OF A BALANCED VEGETARIAN DIET

That said, simply cutting out meat isn't enough it's crucial to make sure you're still getting proper nutrition from other sources. Pay special attention to these nutrients that can be easily missed on a vegetarian diet:

Protein for muscle growth, satiety and energy. Found in beans, lentils, soy products, grains and nuts. As a busy student, you need plenty of protein to fuel your active lifestyle and prevent muscle wasting. Aim for a variety of protein-packed ingredients like tofu, tempeh, edamame, lentils, chickpeas and nutritional yeast at every meal.

Iron for healthy blood and brain function. Found in lentils, cashews, spinach and other leafy greens. Iron deficiency can lead to fatigue and anemia, which is the last thing you need when cramming for finals. Pair iron-rich foods with vitamin C sources like bell peppers, tomatoes and citrus fruits to increase absorption.

Calcium for strong bones. Found in dairy products like milk, yogurt and cheese as well as leafy greens, beans and fortified non-dairy milks. Calcium is essential for maintaining bone density during your bone-building years. If avoiding dairy, opt for calcium-fortified plant milks and load up on cooked greens.

Vitamin B12 for red blood cell formation and neurological function. Primarily found in dairy, eggs and fortified foods like cereals and meat substitutes. B12 deficiency can cause tiredness and anemia. Unless you're taking a B12 supplement, be sure to consume adequate B12 from dairy, eggs, nutritional yeast or fortified plant milks.

Zinc for immune function and wound healing. Found in wheat germ, cashews, chickpeas and oats. Zinc deficiency can impair immunity, which you definitely want to avoid when viruses are spreading in dorms and lecture halls. Sprinkle zinc-rich seeds, nuts or oats over meals.

Omega-3s for brain health. Found in walnuts, flax and chia seeds. These anti-inflammatory fats promote brain function and development. Snack on an omega-3 enriched trail mix or add a spoonful of ground flaxseed or chia to smoothies, oatmeal or baked goods.

The key is to eat a nice variety of fruits, veggies, whole grains, legumes, nuts and seeds at every meal. Snacking smart is important to having nutrient-dense grab-and-go options like homemade energy bites, trail mixes, fresh fruit with nut butter and veggie snack packs can meet your cravings while giving you a nutritional boost.

Variety, balance and planning are so important for vegetarian and vegan students to meet all their nutritional needs. Don't be afraid to take a daily multivitamin to cover your bases either. With these tips in mind, you'll have energy galore to thrive in your studies and social life!

Don't stress about needing fancy equipment or a massive pantry makeover. With just a few basics, you'll have everything you need to whip up delicious veggie dishes in your dorm or apartment kitchen. Here are the essentials to stock your minimalist plant-based kitchen:

Tools

- Chef's knife for chopping veggies a must-have for easy meal prep
- Cutting board go for plastic, wood or flexible cutting mats
- Pots and pans a small and large saucepan, a skillet and a baking sheet will cover most cooking needs
- Can opener, vegetable peeler, spatulas, basic utensils
- Food storage containers for leftovers stock up on reusable containers and mason jars
- Blender or food processor for smoothies, dips and veggie burgers (optional but highly useful)
- Instant Pot or slow cooker for easy, hands-off meals (another terrific time-saving option)

As a student, you likely won't have space for too many unit-taskers. Stick to these versatile basics and you can cook up just about anything. Don't forget a good knife sharpener to keep your blade in tiptop shape!

Pantry Staples

- Oils like olive and vegetable for cooking and making dressings
- Vinegars like balsamic, red wine and apple cider for dressings and marinades
- Canned and dried beans, chickpeas, lentils for protein
- Whole wheat pasta and bread for complex carbs
- Brown rice, quinoa and other whole grains
- Raw nuts, seeds and nut butters for snacking and baking
- Canned tomatoes and tomato paste for sauces and stews
- Vegetable or faux-chicken broth for soups and cooking
- Soy sauce, hot sauce and basic dried spices/herbs
- Dairy or dairy-free milk for smoothies, baking etc.
- Dark chocolate for snacking and baking (every vegetarian need chocolate!)

Stock up on these basics and you'll always have the building blocks for fast, healthy meat-free meals. Canned and frozen produce can also help diversify your veggie intake while sticking to your budget. For more perishable items like fresh fruits and veggies, shop the sales and only buy what you'll consume within a week. Having a few pantry staples and simple tools on hand makes vegetarian meal prep so much easier, even in a tiny kitchen. Get in the habit of batch cooking staples like rice, beans and sauces they keep well and make putting together quick meals a total breeze. With just a little strategy, you'll be a veggie-cooking pro in no time!

BREAKFAST

OVERNIGHT OATS 3 WAYS

Prep: 10 mins | Serves: 1

INGREDIENTS:

- 1/2 cup rolled oats (US) / 50g rolled oats (UK)
- 1/2 cup milk of choice (US) / 120ml milk of choice (UK)
- 1 tablespoon honey or maple syrup
- Optional toppings:
- For Apple Cinnamon: 1/2 apple, diced + 1/4 teaspoon cinnamon
- For Berry Blast: 1/4 cup mixed berries
- For Peanut Butter Banana: 1 tablespoon peanut butter + 1/2 banana, sliced

INSTRUCTIONS:

1. In a jar or container, combine oats, milk, and sweetener.
2. For Apple Cinnamon: Stir in diced apple and cinnamon.
3. For Berry Blast: Add mixed berries.
4. For Peanut Butter Banana: Mix in peanut butter and banana slices.
5. Cover and refrigerate overnight.
6. In the morning, stir and add more milk if desired.
   Nutritional Info (for base recipe): Calories: 250 | Fat: 3g | Carbs: 47g | Protein: 9g
   Student Vegetarian Function: Quick and customizable, great for busy mornings.

TOFU SCRAMBLE

Prep: 10 mins | Cook: 10 mins | Serves: 2

INGREDIENTS:

- 1 block firm tofu, drained and crumbled
- 1 tablespoon olive oil
- 1/2 bell pepper, diced
- 1/2 onion, diced
- 1 teaspoon turmeric
- Salt and pepper, to taste
- Fresh parsley, for garnish

INSTRUCTIONS:

1. Heat olive oil in a skillet over medium heat.
2. Add diced bell pepper and onion. Cook until softened.
3. Add crumbled tofu, turmeric, salt, and pepper.
4. Cook, stirring occasionally, until tofu is heated through and resembles scrambled eggs.
5. Garnish with fresh parsley and serve hot.
   Nutritional Info: Calories: 220 | Fat: 14g | Carbs: 8g | Protein: 18g

BREAKFAST BURRITOS

Prep: 15 mins | Cook: 10 mins | Serves: 2

INGREDIENTS:

- 4 large flour tortillas
- 1 can black beans, drained and rinsed
- 1/2 cup salsa
- 1 avocado, sliced
- 1/2 cup shredded cheese
- Salt and pepper, to taste
- Optional: sour cream or Greek yogurt

INSTRUCTIONS:

1. Warm tortillas in a skillet or microwave.
2. In a bowl, mix black beans, salsa, salt, and pepper.
3. Divide bean mixture, avocado slices, and cheese among tortillas.
4. Roll up each tortilla, folding in the sides.
5. Heat burritos in a skillet until cheese melts.
6. Serve with sour cream or yogurt on the side.
   Nutritional Info: Calories: 480 | Fat: 24g | Carbs: 53g | Protein: 18g

PANCAKES AND WAFFLES

Prep: 10 mins | Cook: 10 mins | Serves: 2-3

INGREDIENTS:

- 1 cup all-purpose flour (US) / 120g plain flour (UK)
- 2 tablespoons sugar
- 1 teaspoon baking powder
- 1/2 teaspoon baking soda
- Pinch of salt
- 1 cup milk of choice (US) / 240ml milk of choice (UK)
- 2 tablespoons melted butter or oil
- 1 teaspoon vanilla extract

INSTRUCTIONS:

1. In a bowl, whisk together flour, sugar, baking powder, baking soda, and salt.
2. In another bowl, mix milk, melted butter or oil, and vanilla extract.
3. Pour wet ingredients into dry ingredients and stir until just combined.
4. Heat a non-stick skillet or waffle iron over medium heat.
5. Pour batter onto skillet or waffle iron and cook until bubbles form.
6. Flip and cook until golden brown.
7. Serve with syrup, fresh fruit, or toppings of choice.
   Nutritional Info (per serving): Calories: 250 | Fat: 9g | Carbs: 36g | Protein: 6g

EASY HOMEMADE GRANOLA

Prep: 10 mins | Cook: 25 mins | Serves: 6

INGREDIENTS:

- 2 cups rolled oats (US) / 200g rolled oats (UK)
- 1/2 cup chopped nuts (e.g., almonds, pecans)
- 1/4 cup honey or maple syrup
- 2 tablespoons coconut oil, melted
- 1 teaspoon vanilla extract
- 1/2 cup dried fruit (e.g., raisins, cranberries)

INSTRUCTIONS:

1. Preheat oven to 300°F (150°C).
2. In a bowl, combine oats and chopped nuts.
3. In a separate bowl, whisk together honey or maple syrup, melted coconut oil, and vanilla extract.
4. Pour wet mixture over oats and nuts, stirring to coat evenly.
5. Spread mixture onto a baking sheet lined with parchment paper.
6. Bake for 20-25 minutes, stirring halfway through, until golden brown.
7. Let granola cool completely, then mix in dried fruit.
8. Store in an airtight container.
   Nutritional Info (per serving): Calories: 280 | Fat: 13g | Carbs: 37g | Protein: 5g
   Student Vegetarian Function: Economical and versatile topping for yogurt or smoothie bowls.

BREAKFAST COOKIES

Prep: 15 mins | Cook: 12 mins | Serves: 12 cookies

INGREDIENTS:

- 2 ripe bananas, mashed
- 1/4 cup peanut butter
- 1/4 cup honey or maple syrup
- 1 teaspoon vanilla extract
- 1 cup rolled oats (US) / 100g rolled oats (UK)
- 1/2 cup dried fruit or chocolate chips
- 1/4 cup chopped nuts (optional)

INSTRUCTIONS:

1. Preheat oven to 350°F (175°C) and line a baking sheet with parchment paper.
2. In a bowl, mix mashed bananas, peanut butter, honey or maple syrup, and vanilla extract.
3. Stir in oats, dried fruit or chocolate chips, and nuts (if using).
4. Scoop spoonsful of dough onto the prepared baking sheet and flatten slightly.
5. Bake for 12 minutes or until golden brown.
6. Let cool on the baking sheet for 5 minutes before transferring to a wire rack to cool completely.
   Nutritional Info (per cookie): Calories: 130 | Fat: 5g | Carbs: 20g | Protein: 3g

AVOCADO TOAST 4 WAYS

Prep: 10 mins | Serves: 2

INGREDIENTS:

- 4 slices whole-grain bread, toasted
- 1 ripe avocado
- Salt and pepper, to taste

VARIATIONS:

1. Classic Avocado Toast: Mash avocado onto toast and season with salt and pepper.
1. Tomato Basil Avocado Toast:
2. Top avocado toast with sliced tomatoes and fresh basil leaves.
3. Everything Bagel Avocado Toast:
4. Sprinkle avocado toast with "everything bagel" seasoning.
5. 4. Sweet and Spicy Avocado Toast:
6. Drizzle avocado toast with honey and a dash of red pepper flakes.
   Nutritional Info (per serving, for classic version): Calories: 200 | Fat: 10g | Carbs: 24g | Protein: 5g
   Student Vegetarian Function: Quick, nutritious, and customizable breakfast option.

BREAKFAST TACOS

Prep: 10 mins | Cook: 10 mins | Serves: 2

INGREDIENTS:

- 4 small flour or corn tortillas
- 4 eggs
- 1/2 bell pepper, diced
- 1/2 onion, diced
- 1/2 cup black beans, drained and rinsed
- 1/2 cup shredded cheese
- Salsa and sliced avocado, for serving
- Salt and pepper, to taste

INSTRUCTIONS:

1. Heat tortillas in a skillet or microwave.
2. In a separate skillet, scramble eggs over medium heat.
3. Add diced bell pepper and onion to the eggs and cook until vegetables are softened.
4. Stir in black beans and shredded cheese until melted.
5. Divide egg mixture among warmed tortillas.
6. Serve with salsa, sliced avocado, and additional toppings if desired.
   Nutritional Info (per serving): Calories: 380 | Fat: 18g | Carbs: 35g | Protein: 21g
   Student Vegetarian Function: Versatile and filling breakfast option that can be made with simple pantry ingredients.

VEGETABLE FRITTATA

Prep: 10 mins | Cook: 20 mins | Serves: 4

INGREDIENTS:

- 6 eggs
- 1/2 cup milk of choice (US) / 120ml milk of choice (UK)
- 1 cup chopped mixed vegetables (e.g., bell peppers, spinach, tomatoes)
- 1/2 cup shredded cheese
- Salt and pepper, to taste
- 1 tablespoon olive oil

INSTRUCTIONS:

1. Preheat oven to 350°F (175°C).
2. In a bowl, whisk together eggs, milk, salt, and pepper.
3. Heat olive oil in an oven-safe skillet over medium heat.
4. Add chopped vegetables and sauté until softened.
5. Pour egg mixture over vegetables in the skillet.
6. Sprinkle shredded cheese on top.
7. Cook on the stove for 3-4 minutes, then transfer to the oven.
8. Bake for 15-18 minutes or until eggs are set.
9. Slice into wedges and serve hot.
   Nutritional Info (per serving): Calories: 220 | Fat: 15g | Carbs: 6g | Protein: 14g
   Student Vegetarian Function: Easy one-pan dish packed with veggies for a balanced breakfast.

BREAKFAST CASSEROLE

Prep: 15 mins | Cook: 40 mins | Serves: 6

INGREDIENTS:

- 6 slices bread, cubed
- 1 cup chopped vegetables (e.g., bell peppers, spinach, onions)
- 1 cup shredded cheese
- 6 eggs
- 1 1/2 cups milk of choice (US) / 360ml milk of choice (UK)
- Salt and pepper, to taste
- Optional: vegetarian sausage or bacon (cooked and chopped)

INSTRUCTIONS:

1. Preheat oven to 350°F (175°C).
2. Grease a baking dish and spread bread cubes evenly.
3. In a bowl, whisk together eggs, milk, salt, and pepper.
4. Stir in chopped vegetables, cheese, and cooked vegetarian sausage or bacon (if using).
5. Pour egg mixture over bread cubes, ensuring even distribution.
6. Cover with foil and bake for 30 minutes.

7. Remove foil and bake for an additional 10 minutes or until golden and set.
8. Let cool slightly before serving.
   Nutritional Info (per serving): Calories: 280 | Fat: 15g | Carbs: 19g | Protein: 17g
   Student Vegetarian Function: Make-ahead dish perfect for breakfast or brunch gatherings.

FRUIT SMOOTHIES

Prep: 5 mins | Serves: 2

INGREDIENTS:

- 1 banana, frozen
- 1 cup mixed frozen fruit (e.g., berries, mango chunks)
- 1 cup milk of choice (US) / 240ml milk of choice (UK)
- 1/2 cup plain Greek yogurt
- 1 tablespoon honey or maple syrup (optional)

INSTRUCTIONS:

1. Combine all ingredients in a blender.
2. Blend until smooth and creamy.
3. Taste and add honey or maple syrup if desired for sweetness.
4. Pour into glasses and serve immediately.
   Nutritional Info (per serving): Calories: 200 | Fat: 3g | Carbs: 38g | Protein: 9g
   Student Vegetarian Function: Quick and refreshing way to start the day with a boost of vitamins.

OVERNIGHT CHIA PUDDINGS

Prep: 5 mins | Chill: Overnight | Serves: 2

INGREDIENTS:

- 1/4 cup chia seeds
- 1 cup milk of choice (US) / 240ml milk of choice (UK)
- 1 tablespoon honey or maple syrup
- 1/2 teaspoon vanilla extract
- Optional toppings: fresh fruit, nuts, coconut flakes

INSTRUCTIONS:

1. In a bowl or jar, whisk together chia seeds, milk, honey or maple syrup, and vanilla extract.
2. Cover and refrigerate overnight or for at least 4 hours.
3. Stir well before serving.
4. Top with fresh fruit, nuts, or coconut flakes if desired.
   Nutritional Info (per serving): Calories: 180 | Fat: 9g | Carbs: 20g | Protein: 6g
   Student Vegetarian Function: Prep in advance for a convenient grab-and-go breakfast.

BREAKFAST BARS

Prep: 15 mins | Cook: 25 mins | Serves: 8 bars

INGREDIENTS:

- 1 1/2 cups rolled oats (US) / 150g rolled oats (UK)
- 1/2 cup chopped nuts or seeds (e.g., almonds, pumpkin seeds)
- 1/2 cup dried fruit (e.g., raisins, cranberries)
- 1/4 cup honey or maple syrup
- 1/4 cup peanut butter or almond butter
- 1 teaspoon vanilla extract
- Pinch of salt

INSTRUCTIONS:

1. Preheat oven to 350°F (175°C) and line a baking dish with parchment paper.
2. In a bowl, combine oats, chopped nuts or seeds, and dried fruit.
3. In a small saucepan, heat honey or maple syrup, peanut butter or almond butter, vanilla extract, and salt until melted and smooth.
4. Pour wet mixture over dry ingredients and mix until well combined.
5. Press mixture firmly into the prepared baking dish.
6. Bake for 20-25 minutes or until golden brown.
7. Let cool completely before cutting into bars.
   Nutritional Info (per bar): Calories: 220 | Fat: 10g | Carbs: 28g | Protein: 6g
   Student Vegetarian Function: Homemade bars for a portable and satisfying breakfast or snack.

EGG MUFFINS

Prep: 10 mins | Cook: 20 mins | Serves: 6 muffins

INGREDIENTS:

- 6 eggs
- 1/2 cup chopped vegetables (e.g., spinach, bell peppers, onions)
- 1/2 cup shredded cheese
- Salt and pepper, to taste
- Cooking spray or olive oil

INSTRUCTIONS:

1. Preheat oven to 350°F (175°C) and grease a muffin tin with cooking spray or olive oil.
2. In a bowl, whisk together eggs, salt, and pepper.
3. Stir in chopped vegetables and shredded cheese.
4. Pour mixture evenly into the muffin tin.
5. Bake for 18-20 minutes or until eggs are set.
6. Let cool slightly before removing from the tin.
   Nutritional Info (per muffin): Calories: 120 | Fat: 8g | Carbs: 2g | Protein: 10g

Student Vegetarian Function: Make-ahead breakfast option that can be customized with your favorite veggies.

BREAKFAST SANDWICHES

Prep: 10 mins | Cook: 5 mins | Serves: 2

INGREDIENTS:

- 4 slices whole-grain bread, toasted
- 4 eggs
- 1/4 cup shredded cheese
- Salt and pepper, to taste
- Optional: sliced avocado, tomato, spinach, or vegetarian sausage patties

INSTRUCTIONS:

1. In a skillet, scramble eggs over medium heat.
2. Season eggs with salt and pepper, then sprinkle shredded cheese on top.
3. Once eggs are cooked and cheese is melted, divide onto toasted bread slices.
4. Add optional toppings like sliced avocado, tomato, spinach, or vegetarian sausage patties.
5. Top with remaining toasted bread slices to make sandwiches.
6. Serve immediately.
   Nutritional Info (per serving): Calories: 320 | Fat: 18g | Carbs: 24g | Protein: 18g
   Student Vegetarian Function: Customizable sandwiches perfect for a satisfying breakfast on busy mornings.

APPETIZERS AND SNACKS

HUMMUS 4 WAYS

Prep: 10 mins | Serves: 4

INGREDIENTS:

- 1 can (15 oz) chickpeas, drained and rinsed
- 1/4 cup tahini
- 2 cloves garlic, minced
- Juice of 1 lemon
- Salt, to taste
- Water, as needed
- Optional add-ins for variations:
- For Roasted Red Pepper Hummus: 1/4 cup roasted red peppers, chopped
- For Spinach and Artichoke Hummus: 1/2 cup cooked spinach, chopped + 1/4 cup chopped artichoke hearts
- For Sun-Dried Tomato Hummus: 1/4 cup sun-dried tomatoes, soaked in hot water and drained
- For Spicy Chipotle Hummus: 1-2 chipotle peppers in adobo sauce (adjust to taste)

INSTRUCTIONS:

1. In a food processor, combine chickpeas, tahini, minced garlic, lemon juice, and salt.
2. Blend until smooth, adding water gradually to achieve desired consistency.
3. For **VARIATIONS:**
1. For Roasted Red Pepper Hummus: Add roasted red peppers and blend until combined.
2. For Spinach and Artichoke Hummus: Stir in cooked spinach and chopped artichoke hearts after blending.
3. For Sun-Dried Tomato Hummus: Blend with soaked sun-dried tomatoes until smooth.
4. For Spicy Chipotle Hummus: Add chipotle peppers and blend until well incorporated.
5. Adjust seasoning if needed and serve with pita bread, veggie sticks, or crackers.
   Nutritional Info (per serving, plain hummus): Calories: 150 | Fat: 8g | Carbs: 16g | Protein: 6g
   Student Vegetarian Function: Versatile and protein-rich dip perfect for snacking or spreading.

SALSA AND GUACAMOLE

Prep: 15 mins | Serves: 4-6

INGREDIENTS:

- For Salsa:
- 4 ripe tomatoes, diced
- 1/2 onion, finely chopped
- 1 jalapeño pepper, seeded and minced
- Juice of 1 lime
- 1/4 cup fresh cilantro, chopped
- Salt and pepper, to taste

For Guacamole:

- 2 ripe avocados
- 1/2 onion, finely chopped
- 1-2 cloves garlic, minced
- Juice of 1 lime
- Salt and pepper, to taste

INSTRUCTIONS:

1. Salsa:

In a bowl, combine diced tomatoes, chopped onion, minced jalapeño, lime juice, cilantro, salt, and pepper. Mix well.

Adjust seasoning to taste and refrigerate until ready to serve.

2. Guacamole:

In a separate bowl, mash avocados with a fork until smooth.

Stir in chopped onion, minced garlic, lime juice, salt, and pepper. Mix until combined.

Taste and adjust seasoning as desired.

Serve salsa and guacamole with tortilla chips or as toppings for tacos, burritos, or salads.

Nutritional Info (per serving, guacamole): Calories: 120 | Fat: 10g | Carbs: 7g | Protein: 2g

Student Vegetarian Function: Quick and fresh dips packed with flavor for easy snacking.

ROASTED CHICKPEAS

Prep: 5 mins | Cook: 30 mins | Serves: 4

INGREDIENTS:

- 2 cans (15 oz each) chickpeas, drained and rinsed
- 2 tablespoons olive oil
- 1 teaspoon smoked paprika
- 1/2 teaspoon cumin
- Salt, to taste

INSTRUCTIONS:

1. Preheat oven to 400°F (200°C).
2. Pat dries the chickpeas with a kitchen towel to remove excess moisture.
3. In a bowl, toss chickpeas with olive oil, smoked paprika, cumin, and salt until evenly coated.
4. Spread chickpeas in a single layer on a baking sheet.
5. Roast in the preheated oven for 25-30 minutes, shaking the pan halfway through, until chickpeas are crispy.
6. Let cool slightly before serving.

Nutritional Info (per serving): Calories: 180 | Fat: 7g | Carbs: 22g | Protein: 7g
Student Vegetarian Function: Crunchy and protein-packed snack alternative to chips.

ROASTED VEGETABLES

Prep: 10 mins | Cook: 25 mins | Serves: 4

INGREDIENTS:

- 2 cups mixed vegetables (e.g., bell peppers, zucchini, cherry tomatoes, red onion)
- 2 tablespoons olive oil
- 2 cloves garlic, minced
- Salt and pepper, to taste
- Fresh herbs (optional), such as rosemary or thyme

INSTRUCTIONS:

1. Preheat oven to 425°F (220°C).
2. In a large bowl, toss mixed vegetables with olive oil, minced garlic, salt, and pepper.
3. Spread vegetables evenly on a baking sheet.
4. Roast in the preheated oven for 20-25 minutes, stirring halfway through, until vegetables are tender and caramelized.
5. Garnish with fresh herbs if desired before serving.
   Nutritional Info (per serving): Calories: 120 | Fat: 7g | Carbs: 14g | Protein: 2g
   Student Vegetarian Function: Easy and flavorful way to enjoy a variety of vegetables as a snack or side dish.

STUFFED MUSHROOMS

Prep: 15 mins | Cook: 20 mins | Serves: 4

INGREDIENTS:

- 16 large button mushrooms
- 1 tablespoon olive oil
- 1 small onion, finely chopped
- 2 cloves garlic, minced
- 1/2 cup breadcrumbs
- 1/4 cup grated Parmesan cheese (or nutritional yeast for vegan option)
- 2 tablespoons chopped fresh parsley
- Salt and pepper, to taste

INSTRUCTIONS:

1. Preheat oven to 375°F (190°C).
2. Remove stems from mushrooms and finely chop them.
3. In a skillet, heat olive oil over medium heat. Add chopped onion and garlic, and sauté until softened.
4. Add chopped mushroom stems to the skillet and cook for 3-4 minutes.

5. Stir in breadcrumbs, Parmesan cheese (or nutritional yeast), chopped parsley, salt, and pepper. Cook for another 2 minutes until mixture is well combined.
6. Remove skillet from heat and let the mixture cool slightly.
7. Spoon the filling into the mushroom caps, pressing gently to pack the filling.
8. Place stuffed mushrooms on a baking sheet and bake for 15-20 minutes until mushrooms are tender and filling is golden brown.
9. Serve hot as a delicious appetizer.
   Nutritional Info (per serving): Calories: 120 | Fat: 5g | Carbs: 15g | Protein: 6g
   Student Vegetarian Function: Elegant and flavorful stuffed mushrooms that are easy to prepare.

VEGETABLE SPRING ROLLS

Prep: 20 mins | Cook: 10 mins | Serves: 4

INGREDIENTS:

- 8 spring roll wrappers
- 2 cups shredded cabbage
- 1 carrot, julienned
- 1 bell pepper, thinly sliced
- 1/2 cucumber, julienned
- 1/4 cup fresh cilantro leaves
- 1/4 cup fresh mint leaves
- Soy sauce or hoisin sauce, for dipping (optional)

INSTRUCTIONS:

1. Prepare all the vegetables and herbs for the filling.
2. Fill a large bowl with warm water.
3. Dip one spring roll wrapper into the water for a few seconds until it softens.
4. Place the wrapper on a clean surface and add a small amount of each vegetable and herbs in the center.
5. Fold the sides of the wrapper over the filling, then roll up tightly.
6. Repeat with remaining wrappers and filling ingredients.
7. Heat a skillet or grill pan over medium heat.
8. Lightly brush each spring roll with oil and cook for 2-3 minutes on each side until golden and crispy.
9. Serve spring rolls with soy sauce or hoisin sauce for dipping.
   Nutritional Info (per serving, 2 rolls): Calories: 150 | Fat: 1g | Carbs: 30g | Protein: 4g
   Student Vegetarian Function: Fresh and light spring rolls perfect for a quick snack or appetizer.

CAPRESE SKEWERS

Prep: 15 mins | Serves: 4

INGREDIENTS:

- 16 cherry tomatoes
- 16 fresh mini mozzarella balls (bocconcini)
- 16 fresh basil leaves
- Balsamic glaze, for drizzling (optional)

- Salt and pepper, to taste

INSTRUCTIONS:

1. Thread cherry tomatoes, mini mozzarella balls, and basil leaves onto small skewers or toothpicks.

2. Arrange the skewers on a serving platter.

3. Drizzle with balsamic glaze if desired.

4. Season with salt and pepper to taste.

5. Serve immediately as a delightful and easy appetizer.

Nutritional Info (per serving): Calories: 120 | Fat: 8g | Carbs: 4g | Protein: 6

Student Vegetarian Function: Simple and elegant finger food for entertaining or snacking.

PIZZAS 4 WAYS

Prep: 15 mins | Cook: 12 mins | Serves: 4

INGREDIENTS:

- 4 small pre-made pizza crusts or flatbreads
- 1/2 cup tomato sauce or pizza sauce
- Assorted toppings (choose from):
- Margherita: Fresh mozzarella, sliced tomatoes, fresh basil leaves
- Veggie Delight: Sliced bell peppers, red onions, mushrooms, olives
- BBQ Chickpea: BBQ sauce, cooked chickpeas, red onion, cilantro
- Pesto Veggie: Pesto sauce, sliced zucchini, cherry tomatoes, pine nuts

INSTRUCTIONS:

1. Preheat oven to 425°F (220°C).
2. Place pizza crusts on a baking sheet.
3. Spread tomato sauce or pizza sauce evenly over each crust.
4. Add desired toppings to each pizza according to the chosen flavor combinations.
5. Bake in the preheated oven for 10-12 minutes or until crust is golden and toppings are heated through.
6. Slice and serve hot as a delicious snack or appetizer.
   Nutritional Info (per serving, Margherita pizza): Calories: 250 | Fat: 8g | Carbs: 35g | Protein: 10g
   Student Vegetarian Function: Quick and customizable mini pizzas for a fun and tasty snack.

QUESADILLAS

Prep: 10 mins | Cook: 10 mins | Serves: 2

INGREDIENTS:

- 4 large flour tortillas
- 1 cup shredded cheese (cheddar, Monterey Jack, or Mexican blend)
- 1 bell pepper, thinly sliced

- 1/2 onion, thinly sliced
- 1 cup cooked black beans
- Optional add-ins: sliced jalapeños, corn kernels, chopped cilantro

INSTRUCTIONS:

1. Heat a skillet over medium heat.
2. Place one tortilla in the skillet and sprinkle half of it with shredded cheese.
3. Layer with sliced bell pepper, onion, black beans, and any desired add-ins.
4. Fold the tortilla in half to cover the filling.
5. Cook for 2-3 minutes on each side until the tortilla is golden and the cheese is melted.
6. Remove from the skillet and repeat with the remaining tortillas and filling ingredients.
7. Cut quesadillas into wedges and serve hot with salsa, guacamole, or sour cream.
   Nutritional Info (per serving): Calories: 400 | Fat: 18g | Carbs: 45g | Protein: 16g
   Student Vegetarian Function: Quick and satisfying snack or light meal that's customizable with favorite ingredients.

NACHOS

Prep: 10 mins | Cook: 10 mins | Serves: 4

INGREDIENTS:

- 1 bag (about 10 oz) tortilla chips
- 1 cup shredded cheese (cheddar or Mexican blend)
- 1/2 cup black beans, drained and rinsed
- 1/2 cup corn kernels (fresh or frozen)
- 1/2 cup diced tomatoes
- Sliced jalapeños, to taste
- Sour cream, salsa, and guacamole, for serving

INSTRUCTIONS:

1. Preheat oven to 375°F (190°C).
2. Spread tortilla chips in a single layer on a baking sheet.
3. Sprinkle shredded cheese evenly over the chips.
4. Scatter black beans, corn kernels, diced tomatoes, and sliced jalapeños over the cheese.
5. Bake in the preheated oven for 8-10 minutes, until cheese is melted and bubbly.
6. Remove from the oven and let cool slightly.
7. Serve nachos hot with sour cream, salsa, and guacamole on the side.
   Nutritional Info (per serving): Calories: 450 | Fat: 25g | Carbs: 45g | Protein: 12g
   Student Vegetarian Function: Easy and crowd-pleasing nachos perfect for sharing with friends.

VEGETABLE SAMOSAS

Prep: 30 mins | Cook: 20 mins | Serves: 4

INGREDIENTS:

- 2 large potatoes, peeled and diced
- 1 cup mixed vegetables (peas, carrots, corn)
- 1 tablespoon vegetable oil
- 1 teaspoon cumin seeds
- 1 teaspoon garam masala
- Salt, to taste
- 12-16 samosa wrappers or spring roll wrappers
- Oil, for frying

INSTRUCTIONS:

1. Boil or steam diced potatoes and mixed vegetables until tender. Drain and set aside.
2. Heat vegetable oil in a skillet over medium heat. Add cumin seeds and sauté until fragrant.
3. Add cooked potatoes, mixed vegetables, garam masala, and salt to the skillet. Stir well to combine and mash lightly.
4. Let the filling cool slightly before assembling the samosas.
5. Take a samosa wrapper and place a spoonful of filling in the center.
6. Fold the wrapper into a triangle, sealing the edges with a little water.
7. Heat oil in a deep skillet or pot over medium-high heat.
8. Fry samosas in batches until golden brown and crispy, about 3-4 minutes per side.
9. Drain on paper towels and serve hot with chutney or dipping sauce.
   Nutritional Info (per serving): Calories: 300 | Fat: 12g | Carbs: 40g | Protein: 6g
   Student Vegetarian Function: Homemade Indian snack with a delicious spiced vegetable filling.

LETTUCE WRAPS

Prep: 15 mins | Cook: 10 mins | Serves: 2-4

INGREDIENTS:

- 1 tablespoon vegetable oil
- 1/2 onion, finely chopped
- 2 cloves garlic, minced
- 1 bell pepper, diced
- 1 carrot, grated
- 1 cup cooked quinoa or rice
- 1/4 cup soy sauce or tamari
- 1 tablespoon rice vinegar
- 1 tablespoon maple syrup or honey
- 1 head iceberg lettuce or butter lettuce, leaves separated

INSTRUCTIONS:

1. Heat vegetable oil in a skillet over medium heat.
2. Add chopped onion and minced garlic, sauté until fragrant.
3. Add diced bell pepper and grated carrot, cook until vegetables are tender.
4. Stir in cooked quinoa or rice.
5. In a small bowl, whisk together soy sauce, rice vinegar, and maple syrup.
6. Pour the sauce over the quinoa mixture and stir well to combine.
7. Spoon the quinoa filling into lettuce leaves, wrap, and secure with toothpicks if needed.
8. Serve lettuce wraps as a light and flavorful snack or appetizer.
   Nutritional Info (per serving): Calories: 250 | Fat: 7g | Carbs: 40g | Protein: 8g
   Student Vegetarian Function: Healthy and satisfying lettuce wraps with a tasty quinoa filling.

ZUCCHINI FRIES

Prep: 15 mins | Cook: 20 mins | Serves: 4

INGREDIENTS:

- 2 medium zucchinis, cut into sticks
- 1/2 cup breadcrumbs
- 1/4 cup grated Parmesan cheese (or nutritional yeast for vegan option)
- 1 teaspoon garlic powder
- 1/2 teaspoon paprika
- Salt and pepper, to taste
- 2 eggs, beaten (or non-dairy milk for vegan option)
- Cooking spray or olive oil

INSTRUCTIONS:

1. Preheat oven to 425°F (220°C). Line a baking sheet with parchment paper.
2. In a shallow bowl, combine breadcrumbs, Parmesan cheese, garlic powder, paprika, salt, and pepper.
3. Dip zucchini sticks into beaten eggs (or non-dairy milk), then coat with breadcrumb mixture.
4. Place coated zucchini sticks on the prepared baking sheet in a single layer.
5. Lightly spray with cooking spray or drizzle with olive oil.
6. Bake for 18-20 minutes, turning halfway through, until zucchini fries are golden and crispy.
7. Serve hot with marinara sauce or ranch dressing for dipping.
   Nutritional Info (per serving): Calories: 150 | Fat: 6g | Carbs: 18g | Protein: 8g
   Student Vegetarian Function: Healthier alternative to traditional fries using zucchini as a tasty snack or side dish.

VEGETABLE FRITTERS

Prep: 20 mins | Cook: 15 mins | Serves: 4

INGREDIENTS:

- 2 cups grated vegetables (zucchini, carrots, sweet potatoes)
- 1/2 cup all-purpose flour (or chickpea flour for gluten-free)

- 1/4 cup grated Parmesan cheese (or nutritional yeast for vegan option)
- 1 teaspoon baking powder
- 2 eggs, beaten (or flaxseed meal + water for vegan option)
- Salt and pepper, to taste
- Olive oil, for frying

INSTRUCTIONS:

1. In a large bowl, combine grated vegetables, flour, Parmesan cheese, baking powder, salt, and pepper.
2. Stir in beaten eggs (or flaxseed meal mixture) until well combined.
3. Heat olive oil in a skillet over medium heat.
4. Drop spoonsful of the vegetable batter into the skillet, flattening slightly with the back of a spoon.
5. Cook for 3-4 minutes on each side until golden brown and crispy.
6. Transfer cooked fritters to a plate lined with paper towels to absorb excess oil.
7. Serve vegetable fritters hot with a dollop of Greek yogurt or sour cream.
   Nutritional Info (per serving): Calories: 180 | Fat: 8g | Carbs: 20g | Protein: 8g
   Student Vegetarian Function: Quick and versatile vegetable fritters using pantry staples for a tasty snack or appetizer.

STUFFED POTATO SKINS

Prep: 15 mins | Cook: 60 mins | Serves: 4

INGREDIENTS:

- 4 large baking potatoes
- 2 tablespoons olive oil
- Salt and pepper, to taste
- 1 cup shredded cheese (cheddar or Mexican blend)
- 1/2 cup sour cream (or Greek yogurt for healthier option)
- 2 green onions, thinly sliced
- Optional add-ins: cooked black beans, diced tomatoes, chopped cilantro

INSTRUCTIONS:

1. Preheat oven to 400°F (200°C).
2. Scrub potatoes clean and pat dry. Prick each potato several times with a fork.
3. Rub potatoes with olive oil and season generously with salt and pepper.
4. Place potatoes directly on oven rack and bake for 45-60 minutes until tender.
5. Remove potatoes from the oven and let cool slightly.
6. Slice each potato in half lengthwise. Scoop out the flesh, leaving a thin layer inside the skins.
7. Place potato skins on a baking sheet. Sprinkle shredded cheese inside each skin.
8. Return to the oven and bake for another 10 minutes until cheese is melted and bubbly.
9. Remove from the oven and top with sour cream, sliced green onions, and any desired add-ins.
10. Serve stuffed potato skins hot as a satisfying appetizer or snack.
    Nutritional Info (per serving): Calories: 300 | Fat: 12g | Carbs: 35g | Protein: 10g
    Student Vegetarian Function: Classic and comforting stuffed potato skins perfect for sharing or enjoying as a meal.

SOUPS, SALADS AND BOWLS

HEARTY VEGETABLE CHILI

Prep: 15 mins | Cook: 30 mins | Serves: 4

INGREDIENTS:

- 1 tablespoon olive oil
- 1 onion, chopped
- 2 garlic cloves, minced
- 1 bell pepper, diced
- 2 carrots, diced
- 1 zucchini, diced
- 1 can (15 oz) diced tomatoes
- 1 can (15 oz) kidney beans, drained and rinsed
- 1 can (15 oz) black beans, drained and rinsed
- 2 tablespoons chili powder
- 1 teaspoon ground cumin
- Salt and pepper, to taste
- Optional toppings: shredded cheese, chopped cilantro, sour cream

INSTRUCTIONS:

1. Heat olive oil in a large pot over medium heat.
2. Add chopped onion and minced garlic. Sauté for 2-3 minutes until fragrant.
3. Add diced bell pepper, carrots, and zucchini to the pot. Cook for 5-6 minutes until vegetables start to soften.
4. Stir in diced tomatoes, kidney beans, and black beans.
5. Season with chili powder, ground cumin, salt, and pepper.
6. Bring to a simmer and cook for 15-20 minutes, stirring occasionally.
7. Taste and adjust seasoning if needed.
8. Serve hot, topped with shredded cheese, chopped cilantro, and a dollop of sour cream if desired.
   Nutritional Info (per serving): Calories: 320 | Fat: 5g | Carbs: 58g | Protein: 15g
   Student Vegetarian Function: Quick and nutritious one-pot meal packed with protein and fiber.

COMFORTING LENTIL SOUP

Prep: 10 mins | Cook: 30 mins | Serves: 4

INGREDIENTS:

- 1 tablespoon olive oil
- 1 onion, diced
- 2 carrots, diced
- 2 celery stalks, diced
- 2 garlic cloves, minced
- 1 cup dried lentils, rinsed

- 4 cups vegetable broth
- 1 can (15 oz) diced tomatoes
- 1 teaspoon dried thyme
- Salt and pepper, to taste
- Fresh parsley, for garnish

INSTRUCTIONS:

1. Heat olive oil in a pot over medium heat.
2. Add diced onion, carrots, celery, and minced garlic. Sauté for 5-6 minutes until vegetables are tender.
3. Stir in rinsed lentils, vegetable broth, diced tomatoes, and dried thyme.
4. Bring to a boil, then reduce heat to low and simmer for 25-30 minutes until lentils are cooked and soup has thickened.
5. Season with salt and pepper to taste.
6. Garnish with fresh parsley before serving.
   Nutritional Info (per serving): Calories: 280 | Fat: 4g | Carbs: 45g | Protein: 18g
   Student Vegetarian Function: Easy-to-make and protein-rich soup perfect for chilly days.

CLASSIC MINESTRONE SOUP

Prep: 15 mins | Cook: 30 mins | Serves: 4

INGREDIENTS:

- 1 tablespoon olive oil
- 1 onion, chopped
- 2 garlic cloves, minced
- 2 carrots, diced
- 2 celery stalks, diced
- 1 zucchini, diced
- 1 can (15 oz) diced tomatoes
- 4 cups vegetable broth
- 1 can (15 oz) cannellini beans, drained and rinsed
- 1 cup small pasta (e.g., ditalini or elbow)
- 1 teaspoon dried basil
- Salt and pepper, to taste
- Grated Parmesan cheese, for serving (optional)

INSTRUCTIONS:

1. Heat olive oil in a large pot over medium heat.
2. Add chopped onion and minced garlic. Sauté for 2-3 minutes until fragrant.
3. Add diced carrots, celery, and zucchini. Cook for 5-6 minutes until vegetables start to soften.
4. Stir in diced tomatoes, vegetable broth, and cannellini beans.
5. Bring to a boil, then add pasta and dried basil.
6. Reduce heat to medium-low and simmer for 12-15 minutes until pasta is tender.
7. Season with salt and pepper to taste.
8. Serve hot, topped with grated Parmesan cheese if desired.

Nutritional Info (per serving): Calories: 320 | Fat: 5g | Carbs: 58g | Protein: 15g
Student Vegetarian Function: A classic Italian soup loaded with veggies, beans, and pasta for a satisfying meal.

FRESH GREEK SALAD

Prep: 15 mins | Serves: 4

INGREDIENTS:

- 2 large tomatoes, diced
- 1 cucumber, diced
- 1/2 red onion, thinly sliced
- 1 bell pepper, diced
- 1/2 cup Kalamata olives, pitted
- 1/2 cup feta cheese, crumbled
- Fresh oregano leaves (or dried oregano)
- Salt and pepper, to taste
- 2 tablespoons olive oil
- Juice of 1 lemon

INSTRUCTIONS:

1. In a large bowl, combine diced tomatoes, cucumber, red onion, bell pepper, and Kalamata olives.
2. Sprinkle crumbled feta cheese and fresh oregano leaves over the vegetables.
3. Season with salt and pepper.
4. Drizzle olive oil and freshly squeezed lemon juice over the salad.
5. Toss gently to combine all ingredients.
6. Serve immediately as a refreshing side salad or light meal.
   Nutritional Info (per serving): Calories: 180 | Fat: 12g | Carbs: 15g | Protein: 5g
   Student Vegetarian Function: A classic Mediterranean salad bursting with flavors and textures.

CRUNCHY TACO SALAD

Prep: 15 mins | Serves: 4

INGREDIENTS:

- 1 head romaine lettuce, chopped
- 1 cup cherry tomatoes, halved
- 1/2 red onion, thinly sliced
- 1 bell pepper, diced
- 1 cup cooked black beans
- 1 cup corn kernels (fresh or frozen)
- 1 avocado, diced
- 1/2 cup tortilla chips, crushed
- 1/2 cup shredded cheddar cheese (or vegan cheese)
- 1/4 cup cilantro, chopped
- 1/4 cup salsa

- 1/4 cup sour cream (or Greek yogurt)
- Lime wedges, for serving
- Salt and pepper, to taste

INSTRUCTIONS:

1. In a large bowl, combine chopped romaine lettuce, cherry tomatoes, red onion, bell pepper, black beans, corn kernels, avocado, crushed tortilla chips, shredded cheddar cheese, and chopped cilantro.
2. Drizzle salsa and sour cream over the salad.
3. Season with salt and pepper to taste.
4. Toss gently to coat all ingredients.
5. Serve immediately, with lime wedges on the side for extra zest.
   Nutritional Info (per serving): Calories: 350 | Fat: 18g | Carbs: 40g | Protein: 12g
   Student Vegetarian Function: A satisfying and flavorful taco-inspired salad loaded with veggies and protein.

COLORFUL BUDDHA BOWL

Prep: 15 mins | Cook: 20 mins | Serves: 2

INGREDIENTS:

- 1 cup cooked quinoa or brown rice
- 1 cup chickpeas, drained and rinsed
- 1 small sweet potato, cubed
- 1 cup broccoli florets
- 1/2 cup shredded purple cabbage
- 1 avocado, sliced
- 2 tablespoons tahini (or other dressing of choice)
- Salt and pepper, to taste
- Fresh lemon wedges, for serving

INSTRUCTIONS:

1. Preheat the oven to 400°F (200°C).
2. Toss cubed sweet potato and broccoli florets with olive oil, salt, and pepper on a baking sheet.
3. Roast in the oven for 20 minutes or until tender and lightly browned.
4. Meanwhile, assemble the Buddha bowl by dividing cooked quinoa or brown rice between two bowls.
5. Arrange roasted sweet potato, broccoli, chickpeas, shredded cabbage, and avocado slices on top of the grains.
6. Drizzle tahini or dressing over the bowl.
7. Season with additional salt and pepper if desired.
8. Serve with fresh lemon wedges for squeezing over the bowl.
   Nutritional Info (per serving): Calories: 480 | Fat: 20g | Carbs: 62g | Protein: 16
   Student Vegetarian Function: A vibrant and balanced bowl packed with nutrients and flavors.

DIY BURRITO BOWL

Prep: 15 mins | Cook: 15 mins | Serves: 2

INGREDIENTS:

- 1 cup cooked brown rice or cilantro-lime rice
- 1 cup black beans, drained and rinsed
- 1 cup corn kernels (fresh or frozen)
- 1 bell pepper, diced
- 1/2 red onion, diced
- 1 avocado, sliced
- Fresh cilantro, chopped
- Salsa or Pico de Gallo
- Lime wedges, for serving
- Salt and pepper, to taste

INSTRUCTIONS:

1. In a bowl, combine cooked rice, black beans, corn kernels, diced bell pepper, and red onion.
2. Toss gently to mix all ingredients.
3. Divide the mixture into serving bowls.
4. Top with sliced avocado, chopped cilantro, and salsa or Pico de Gallo.
5. Season with salt and pepper to taste.
6. Serve with lime wedges for squeezing over the bowl.
   Nutritional Info (per serving): Calories: 420 | Fat: 18g | Carbs: 58g | Protein: 12g
   Student Vegetarian Function: Build-your-own burrito bowl with customizable toppings for a satisfying meal.

VIBRANT PASTA SALAD

Prep: 10 mins | Cook: 10 mins | Serves: 4

INGREDIENTS:

- 8 oz pasta (penne, fusilli, or your choice)
- 1 cup cherry tomatoes, halved
- 1/2 cucumber, diced
- 1/4 red onion, thinly sliced
- 1/2 bell pepper, diced
- 1/4 cup black olives, sliced
- 1/4 cup feta cheese, crumbled (optional)
- 2 tablespoons chopped fresh basil
- 3 tablespoons olive oil
- 2 tablespoons red wine vinegar
- Salt and pepper, to taste

INSTRUCTIONS:

1. Cook pasta according to package instructions. Drain and rinse under cold water.
2. In a large bowl, combine cooked pasta, cherry tomatoes, cucumber, red onion, bell pepper, black olives, feta cheese, and chopped basil.
3. In a small bowl, whisk together olive oil, red wine vinegar, salt, and pepper to make the dressing.
4. Pour the dressing over the pasta salad and toss to coat evenly.
5. Adjust seasoning if needed.
6. Serve immediately or refrigerate until ready to serve.
   Nutritional Info (per serving): Calories: 350 | Fat: 14g | Carbs: 48g | Protein: 10g
   Student Vegetarian Function: Easy-to-make pasta salad that's perfect for meal prep and packed lunches.

REFRESHING QUINOA TABBOULEH

Prep: 15 mins | Cook: 15 mins | Serves: 4

INGREDIENTS:

- 1 cup cooked quinoa
- 1 cucumber, finely diced
- 2 tomatoes, finely diced
- 1/2 red onion, finely chopped
- 1/2 cup fresh parsley, chopped
- 1/4 cup fresh mint leaves, chopped
- Juice of 2 lemons
- 3 tablespoons olive oil
- Salt and pepper, to taste

INSTRUCTIONS:

1. In a large bowl, combine cooked quinoa, diced cucumber, tomatoes, red onion, parsley, and mint leaves.
2. In a small bowl, whisk together lemon juice, olive oil, salt, and pepper to make the dressing.
3. Pour the dressing over the quinoa mixture and toss to combine.
4. Adjust seasoning if needed.
5. Refrigerate for at least 30 minutes to allow flavors to meld.
6. Serve chilled as a refreshing and nutritious salad.
   Nutritional Info (per serving): Calories: 240 | Fat: 12g | Carbs: 30g | Protein: 6g
   Student Vegetarian Function: A Middle Eastern-inspired salad with protein-rich quinoa and fresh herbs.

BEAN AND COUSCOUS SALAD

Prep: 15 mins | Cook: 10 mins | Serves: 4

INGREDIENTS:

- 1 cup couscous
- 1 can (15 oz) mixed beans, drained and rinsed
- 1 bell pepper, diced
- 1/2 red onion, finely chopped

- 1/2 cup cherry tomatoes, halved
- 1/4 cup chopped fresh parsley
- Juice of 1 lemon
- 3 tablespoons olive oil
- Salt and pepper, to taste

INSTRUCTIONS:

1. Prepare couscous according to package instructions. Fluff with a fork and let cool.
2. In a large bowl, combine cooked couscous, mixed beans, diced bell pepper, red onion, cherry tomatoes, and choppod parolcy.
3. In a small bowl, whisk together lemon juice, olive oil, salt, and pepper to make the dressing.
4. Pour the dressing over the salad and toss to coat evenly.
5. Adjust seasoning if needed.
6. Serve chilled or at room temperature.
   Nutritional Info (per serving): Calories: 320 | Fat: 12g | Carbs: 45g | Protein: 10g
   Student Vegetarian Function: Quick and versatile salad packed with fiber and protein from beans and couscous.

CLASSIC POTATO SALAD

Prep: 15 mins | Cook: 15 mins | Serves: 4

INGREDIENTS:

- 4 medium potatoes, peeled and diced
- 1/2 cup mayonnaise (or vegan mayo)
- 1 tablespoon Dijon mustard
- 2 celery stalks, finely chopped
- 1/4 cup finely chopped red onion
- 2 tablespoons chopped fresh dill (or dried dill)
- Salt and pepper, to taste

INSTRUCTIONS:

1. Place diced potatoes in a pot and cover with cold water. Bring to a boil, then reduce heat and simmer for 10-12 minutes until potatoes are tender but still firm.
2. Drain cooked potatoes and let cool slightly.
3. In a large bowl, combine mayonnaise, Dijon mustard, chopped celery, red onion, and chopped dill.
4. Add cooked potatoes to the bowl and toss gently to coat with the dressing.
5. Season with salt and pepper to taste.
6. Refrigerate for at least 1 hour before serving to allow flavors to develop.
7. Serve chilled as a classic side dish or light meal.
   Nutritional Info (per serving): Calories: 280 | Fat: 15g | Carbs: 30g | Protein: 4g
   Student Vegetarian Function: Creamy and satisfying potato salad that's perfect for picnics and gatherings.

SOBA NOODLE SALAD WITH PEANUT DRESSING

Prep: 15 mins | Cook: 8 mins | Serves: 4

INGREDIENTS:

- 8 oz soba noodles
- 1 bell pepper, thinly sliced
- 1 cucumber, julienned
- 2 carrots, julienned
- 1/4 cup chopped green onions
- 1/4 cup chopped cilantro
- 1/4 cup chopped peanuts
- Sesame seeds, for garnish

For Peanut Dressing:

- 1/4 cup creamy peanut butter
- 2 tablespoons soy sauce
- 2 tablespoons rice vinegar
- 1 tablespoon honey (or maple syrup for vegan option)
- 1 clove garlic, minced
- 1 teaspoon grated ginger
- Water, as needed

INSTRUCTIONS:

1. Cook soba noodles according to package instructions. Drain and rinse under cold water.
2. In a large bowl, combine cooked soba noodles, sliced bell pepper, julienned cucumber, julienned carrots, chopped green onions, and chopped cilantro.
3. In a separate bowl, whisk together peanut butter, soy sauce, rice vinegar, honey, minced garlic, and grated ginger to make the dressing.
4. Add water gradually to the dressing to achieve desired consistency.
5. Pour the peanut dressing over the noodle salad and toss to coat evenly.
6. Garnish with chopped peanuts and sesame seeds.
7. Serve chilled or at room temperature.
   Nutritional Info (per serving): Calories: 380 | Fat: 14g | Carbs: 54g | Protein: 14g
   Student Vegetarian Function: Flavorful and protein-packed noodle salad with a creamy peanut dressing.

FARRO AND KALE SALAD WITH LEMON DRESSING

Prep: 15 mins | Cook: 20 mins | Serves: 4

INGREDIENTS:

- 1 cup farro
- 1 bunch kale, stems removed and leaves thinly sliced
- 1/4 cup dried cranberries
- 1/4 cup chopped walnuts

- 1/4 cup crumbled feta cheese (optional)

For Lemon Dressing:

- Juice of 2 lemons
- 1/4 cup olive oil
- 1 tablespoon Dijon mustard
- 1 tablespoon honey (or maple syrup for vegan option)
- Salt and pepper, to taste

INSTRUCTIONS:

1. Cook farro according to package instructions. Drain and let cool.
2. In a large bowl, massage kale leaves with a bit of olive oil to soften.
3. Add cooked farro, dried cranberries, chopped walnuts, and crumbled feta cheese (if using) to the bowl.
4. In a small bowl, whisk together lemon juice, olive oil, Dijon mustard, honey, salt, and pepper to make the dressing.
5. Pour the lemon dressing over the salad and toss to combine.
6. Adjust seasoning if needed.
7. Serve immediately or refrigerate until ready to serve.
   Nutritional Info (per serving): Calories: 350 | Fat: 18g | Carbs: 45g | Protein: 8g
   Student Vegetarian Function: Nutrient-rich salad featuring hearty farro and kale with a zesty lemon dressing.

TANGY 3 BEAN SALAD

Prep: 10 mins | Serves: 4

INGREDIENTS:

- 1 can (15 oz) kidney beans, drained and rinsed
- 1 can (15 oz) cannellini beans, drained and rinsed
- 1 can (15 oz) black beans, drained and rinsed
- 1 bell pepper, diced
- 1/2 red onion, finely chopped
- 1/4 cup chopped fresh parsley
- 1/4 cup olive oil
- 2 tablespoons red wine vinegar
- 1 tablespoon Dijon mustard
- Salt and pepper, to taste

INSTRUCTIONS:

1. In a large bowl, combine kidney beans, cannellini beans, black beans, diced bell pepper, chopped red onion, and chopped parsley.
2. In a small bowl, whisk together olive oil, red wine vinegar, Dijon mustard, salt, and pepper to make the dressing.
3. Pour the dressing over the bean mixture and toss to coat evenly.

4. Adjust seasoning if needed.
5. Serve chilled or at room temperature.
    Nutritional Info (per serving): Calories: 320 | Fat: 14g | Carbs: 40g | Protein: 15g
    Student Vegetarian Function: A protein-packed and flavorful bean salad that's perfect for meal prep.

LEMON HERB LENTIL SALAD

Prep: 10 mins | Cook: 20 mins | Serves: 4

INGREDIENTS:

- 1 cup green or brown lentils
- 1 cucumber, diced
- 1 bell pepper, diced
- 1/4 cup chopped fresh parsley
- 2 tablespoons chopped fresh mint
- Juice of 2 lemons
- 3 tablespoons olive oil
- Salt and pepper, to taste

INSTRUCTIONS:

1. Cook lentils according to package instructions. Drain and let cool.
2. In a large bowl, combine cooked lentils, diced cucumber, diced bell pepper, chopped parsley, and chopped mint.
3. In a small bowl, whisk together lemon juice, olive oil, salt, and pepper to make the dressing.
4. Pour the lemon dressing over the lentil salad and toss to combine.
5. Adjust seasoning if needed.
6. Serve chilled or at room temperature.
    Nutritional Info (per serving): Calories: 280 | Fat: 12g | Carbs: 35g | Protein: 14g
    Student Vegetarian Function: A light and refreshing lentil salad bursting with lemony herb flavors.

SANDWICHES, WRAPS AND TACOS

GOURMET GRILLED CHEESE

Prep: 5 mins | Cook: 10 mins | Serves: 2

INGREDIENTS:

- 4 slices of bread (whole wheat or sourdough)
- 1 cup shredded cheese (cheddar, mozzarella, or your favorite)
- 2 tablespoons butter
- Optional add-ins: sliced tomato, caramelized onions, spinach, or avocado

INSTRUCTIONS:

1. Heat a skillet or griddle over medium heat.
2. Butter one side of each slice of bread.
3. Place two slices of bread, buttered side down, on the skillet.
4. Layer shredded cheese (and any desired add-ins) on top of the bread slices.
5. Top with the remaining slices of bread, buttered side up.
6. Cook for 3-4 minutes on each side until the bread is golden brown and the cheese is melted.
7. Slice diagonally and serve hot.
   Nutritional Info (per serving): Calories: 400 | Fat: 24g | Carbs: 30g | Protein: 16g
   Student Vegetarian Function: Quick and customizable grilled cheese perfect for a satisfying lunch or dinner.

ULTIMATE VEGGIE BURGER

Prep: 15 mins | Cook: 10 mins | Serves: 4

INGREDIENTS:

- 1 can (15 oz) black beans, drained and rinsed
- 1/2 cup breadcrumbs
- 1/4 cup grated carrots
- 1/4 cup finely chopped onion
- 1 clove garlic, minced
- 1 teaspoon smoked paprika
- Salt and pepper, to taste
- Burger buns
- Toppings: lettuce, tomato, pickles, avocado, cheese

INSTRUCTIONS:

1. In a mixing bowl, mash black beans using a fork or potato masher.
2. Add breadcrumbs, grated carrots, chopped onion, minced garlic, smoked paprika, salt, and pepper. Mix until well combined.
3. Divide the mixture into four portions and shape into burger patties.

4. Heat a non-stick skillet or grill pan over medium heat.
5. Cook veggie burger patties for 4-5 minutes on each side until golden brown and heated through.
6. Toast burger buns on the skillet for 1-2 minutes.
7. Assemble burgers with lettuce, tomato, pickles, avocado, and cheese.
8. Serve hot with your favorite condiments.
   Nutritional Info (per serving): Calories: 350 | Fat: 8g | Carbs: 55g | Protein: 15g
   Student Vegetarian Function: Homemade veggie burgers packed with plant-based protein and fiber.

FLAVORFUL VEGGIE GYROS

Prep: 15 mins | Cook: 10 mins | Serves: 2

INGREDIENTS:

- 4 pita breads
- 1 cup sliced cucumber
- 1 cup cherry tomatoes, halved
- 1/2 red onion, thinly sliced
- 1 cup shredded lettuce or cabbage
- 1/2 cup tzatziki sauce (store-bought or homemade)
- Optional: crumbled feta cheese, olives, roasted red peppers

INSTRUCTIONS:

1. Warm pita breads in a toaster oven or microwave.
2. In a bowl, combine sliced cucumber, cherry tomatoes, red onion, and shredded lettuce.
3. Spread tzatziki sauce inside each pita bread.
4. Fill pitas with the vegetable mixture.
5. Add optional toppings like crumbled feta cheese, olives, or roasted red peppers if desired.
6. Serve immediately as a delicious and satisfying gyro wrap.
   Nutritional Info (per serving): Calories: 350 | Fat: 12g | Carbs: 50g | Protein: 10g
   Student Vegetarian Function: Quick and tasty vegetarian gyros filled with fresh veggies and creamy tzatziki sauce.

HOMEMADE FALAFEL WRAPS

Prep: 20 mins | Cook: 10 mins | Serves: 4

INGREDIENTS:

- 1 can (15 oz) chickpeas, drained and rinsed
- 1/4 cup chopped fresh parsley
- 1/4 cup chopped fresh cilantro
- 2 cloves garlic, minced
- 1 teaspoon ground cumin
- 1 teaspoon ground coriander
- Salt and pepper, to taste
- 2 tablespoons all-purpose flour
- 2 tablespoons olive oil

- 4 whole wheat wraps
- Sliced cucumber, tomato, lettuce, and tahini sauce (for serving)

INSTRUCTIONS:

1. In a food processor, combine chickpeas, chopped parsley, chopped cilantro, minced garlic, ground cumin, ground coriander, salt, and pepper.
2. Pulse until the mixture is coarse and well combined.
3. Transfer the mixture to a bowl and stir in all-purpose flour to help bind.
4. Shape the mixture into small patties.
5. Heat olive oil in a skillet over medium heat.
6. Cook falafel patties for 3-4 minutes on each side until golden brown and crispy.
7. Warm whole wheat wraps in a skillet or microwave.
8. Assemble wraps with falafel patties, sliced cucumber, tomato, lettuce, and drizzle with tahini sauce.
9. Roll up wraps tightly and serve immediately.
   Nutritional Info (per serving): Calories: 380 | Fat: 14g | Carbs: 50g | Protein: 14g
   Student Vegetarian Function: Easy-to-make falafel wraps filled with Middle Eastern flavors and textures.

VEGGIE FAJITA WRAPS

Prep: 15 mins | Cook: 15 mins | Serves: 4

INGREDIENTS:

- 2 bell peppers, thinly sliced
- 1 onion, thinly sliced
- 1 zucchini, sliced into strips
- 1 cup sliced mushrooms
- 2 tablespoons fajita seasoning
- 2 tablespoons olive oil
- 8 whole wheat tortillas
- Optional toppings: salsa, guacamole, sour cream, shredded cheese

INSTRUCTIONS:

1. Heat olive oil in a skillet over medium-high heat.
2. Add sliced bell peppers, onion, zucchini, and mushrooms to the skillet.
3. Sprinkle fajita seasoning over the vegetables and toss to coat.
4. Cook for 8-10 minutes until vegetables are tender and lightly charred.
5. Warm whole wheat tortillas in a dry skillet or microwave.
6. Divide the cooked vegetables among the tortillas.
7. Add optional toppings like salsa, guacamole, sour cream, or shredded cheese.
8. Roll up tortillas and serve hot as flavorful veggie fajita wraps.
   Nutritional Info (per serving): Calories: 320 | Fat: 12g |Carbs: 45g | Protein: 10g
   Student Vegetarian Function: Quick and colorful veggie fajitas wrapped in whole wheat tortillas.

LETTUCE WRAP SANDWICHES

Prep: 15 mins | Serves: 2

INGREDIENTS:

- Large lettuce leaves (such as romaine or butterhead)
- 1 cup cooked quinoa or rice
- 1/2 cup diced bell peppers
- 1/2 cup shredded carrots
- 1/4 cup sliced cucumber
- 1/4 cup hummus or mashed avocado
- Optional: sliced tofu, tempeh, or chickpeas for added protein
- Salt and pepper, to taste

INSTRUCTIONS:

1. Wash and dry large lettuce leaves, then lay them flat on a cutting board.
2. In the center of each lettuce leaf, layer cooked quinoa or rice, diced bell peppers, shredded carrots, sliced cucumber, and a dollop of hummus or mashed avocado.
3. Add optional protein like sliced tofu, tempeh, or chickpeas if desired.
4. Season with salt and pepper to taste.
5. Fold the sides of the lettuce leaf over the filling and roll up tightly to create a wrap.
6. Secure with toothpicks if needed and serve immediately.
   Nutritional Info (per serving): Calories: 250 | Fat: 8g | Carbs: 38g | Protein: 10g
   Student Vegetarian Function: Fresh and satisfying lettuce wrap sandwiches filled with nutritious ingredients.

CLASSIC VEGGIE SANDWICH

Prep: 10 mins | Serves: 1

INGREDIENTS:

- 2 slices whole grain bread
- 2 tablespoons hummus or cream cheese
- 1/4 cup shredded lettuce
- 1/4 cup sliced cucumber
- 1/4 cup sliced bell peppers
- 2-3 slices tomato
- 1-2 tablespoons sliced olives or pickles
- Salt and pepper, to taste

INSTRUCTIONS:

1. Spread hummus or cream cheese evenly on one side of each slice of bread.
2. Layer shredded lettuce, sliced cucumber, bell peppers, tomato slices, and sliced olives or pickles on one slice of bread.
3. Season with salt and pepper to taste.

4. Place the second slice of bread on top to form a sandwich.
5. Slice in half diagonally and serve immediately.
   Nutritional Info (per serving): Calories: 300 | Fat: 8g | Carbs: 48g | Protein: 12g
   Student Vegetarian Function: Simple and nutritious veggie sandwich that's perfect for a quick lunch.

FLAVORFUL VEGGIE TACOS

Prep: 15 mins | Cook: 10 mins | Serves: 2

INGREDIENTS:

- 4 small corn or flour tortillas
- 1 cup cooked black beans or refried beans
- 1 cup diced bell peppers (mixed colors)
- 1/2 cup diced red onion
- 1 tablespoon taco seasoning
- Optional toppings: salsa, guacamole, shredded lettuce, chopped cilantro, lime wedges

INSTRUCTIONS:

1. Warm tortillas in a dry skillet or microwave.
2. In a separate skillet, heat a bit of olive oil over medium heat.
3. Add diced bell peppers and red onion to the skillet, then sprinkle taco seasoning over the vegetables.
4. Cook for 5-7 minutes until vegetables are tender and fragrant.
5. Warm black beans or refried beans in a saucepan or microwave.
6. Spread beans evenly on each tortilla.
7. Top with cooked bell peppers and red onion.
8. Add optional toppings like salsa, guacamole, shredded lettuce, chopped cilantro, and a squeeze of lime juice.
9. Fold or roll up tortillas and serve immediately.
   Nutritional Info (per serving): Calories: 320 | Fat: 5g | Carbs: 58g | Protein: 12g
   Student Vegetarian Function: Quick and tasty veggie tacos loaded with flavor and texture.

PORTOBELLO MUSHROOM SANDWICH

Prep: 10 mins | Cook: 10 mins | Serves: 2

INGREDIENTS:

- 2 large portobello mushroom caps
- 2 tablespoons balsamic vinegar
- 2 tablespoons olive oil
- Salt and pepper, to taste
- 4 slices whole grain bread
- 2 tablespoons hummus or pesto
- 1/2 cup baby spinach or arugula
- Sliced tomato and red onion (optional)

INSTRUCTIONS:

1. Clean portobello mushroom caps and remove stems.
2. In a shallow dish, whisk together balsamic vinegar, olive oil, salt, and pepper.
3. Brush both sides of mushroom caps with the balsamic mixture.
4. Heat a grill pan or skillet over medium heat.
5. Cook mushroom caps for 4-5 minutes on each side until tender and slightly charred.
6. Toast whole grain bread slices.
7. Spread hummus or pesto on one side of each bread slice.
8. Layer baby spinach or arugula, grilled portobello mushroom caps, and optional sliced tomato and red onion on the bread slices.
9. Top with remaining bread slices to form sandwiches.
10. Slice in half diagonally and serve warm.
    Nutritional Info (per serving): Calories: 280 | Fat: 12g | Carbs: 35g | Protein: 10g
    Student Vegetarian Function: Hearty portobello mushroom sandwiches with bold flavors and a satisfying texture.

POTATO TACOS

Prep: 15 mins | Cook: 20 mins | Serves: 4

INGREDIENTS:

- 4 small potatoes, diced
- 1 tablespoon olive oil
- 1 teaspoon chili powder
- 1/2 teaspoon cumin
- Salt and pepper, to taste
- 8 small corn tortillas
- Toppings: shredded lettuce, diced tomatoes, salsa, avocado slices, hot sauce

INSTRUCTIONS:

1. Preheat oven to 400°F (200°C).
2. Toss diced potatoes with olive oil, chili powder, cumin, salt, and pepper.
3. Spread potatoes in a single layer on a baking sheet.
4. Roast in the oven for 15-20 minutes until potatoes are tender and crispy.
5. Warm corn tortillas in a dry skillet or microwave.
6. Divide roasted potatoes evenly among the tortillas.
7. Top with shredded lettuce, diced tomatoes, salsa, avocado slices, and hot sauce.
8. Fold or roll up tortillas and serve immediately.
   Nutritional Info (per serving): Calories: 280 | Fat: 5g | Carbs: 50g | Protein: 6g
   Student Vegetarian Function: Delicious and filling potato tacos with crispy roasted potatoes and flavorful toppings.

LENTIL SLOPPY JOES

Prep: 10 mins | Cook: 20 mins | Serves: 4

INGREDIENTS:

- 1 cup cooked lentils
- 1 tablespoon olive oil
- 1 small onion, finely chopped
- 1 bell pepper, diced
- 2 cloves garlic, minced
- 1 can (15 oz) tomato sauce
- 2 tablespoons tomato paste
- 1 tablespoon maple syrup or brown sugar
- 1 tablespoon Worcestershire sauce (vegetarian-friendly)
- 1 tablespoon Dijon mustard
- Salt and pepper, to taste
- Hamburger buns or sandwich rolls

INSTRUCTIONS:

1. Heat olive oil in a skillet over medium heat.
2. Add chopped onion and bell pepper, and sauté until softened, about 5 minutes.
3. Add minced garlic and cook for another 1-2 minutes.
4. Stir in cooked lentils, tomato sauce, tomato paste, maple syrup (or brown sugar), Worcestershire sauce, Dijon mustard, salt, and pepper.
5. Simmer for 10-15 minutes until the mixture thickens and flavors meld together.
6. Toast hamburger buns or sandwich rolls if desired.
7. Spoon lentil mixture onto the buns to make sloppy joe sandwiches.
8. Serve hot with your favorite side dishes.
   Nutritional Info (per serving): Calories: 300 | Fat: 4g | Carbs: 55g | Protein: 14g
   Student Vegetarian Function: A meatless twist on the classic sloppy joe sandwich, made with hearty lentils and savory sauce.

ROASTED VEGETABLE SANDWICH

Prep: 15 mins | Cook: 20 mins | Serves: 2

INGREDIENTS:

- 1 zucchini, sliced lengthwise
- 1 red bell pepper, sliced
- 1 small eggplant, sliced
- 2 tablespoons olive oil
- Salt and pepper, to taste
- 4 slices whole grain bread
- 2 tablespoons hummus or pesto
- Handful of baby spinach or arugula

INSTRUCTIONS:

1. Preheat oven to 400°F (200°C).
2. Toss sliced zucchini, red bell pepper, and eggplant with olive oil, salt, and pepper.
3. Spread vegetables in a single layer on a baking sheet.
4. Roast in the oven for 15-20 minutes until vegetables are tender and lightly caramelized.
5. Toast whole grain bread slices.
6. Spread hummus or pesto on one side of each bread slice.
7. Layer roasted vegetables and fresh baby spinach or arugula on the bread slices.
8. Top with remaining bread slices to form sandwiches.
9. Slice in half diagonally and serve warm.
   Nutritional Info (per serving): Calories: 320 | Fat: 14g | Carbs: 40g | Protein: 10g
   Student Vegetarian Function: A satisfying roasted vegetable sandwich bursting with flavors and textures.

BLACK BEAN AND SWEET POTATO TACOS

Prep: 15 mins | Cook: 20 mins | Serves: 4

INGREDIENTS:

- 1 large sweet potato, peeled and diced
- 1 tablespoon olive oil
- 1 can (15 oz) black beans, drained and rinsed
- 1 teaspoon chili powder
- 1/2 teaspoon cumin
- Salt and pepper, to taste
- 8 small corn or flour tortillas
- Toppings: diced avocado, salsa, shredded cabbage or lettuce, lime wedges

INSTRUCTIONS:

1. Preheat oven to 400°F (200°C).
2. Toss diced sweet potato with olive oil, chili powder, cumin, salt, and pepper.
3. Spread sweet potato in a single layer on a baking sheet.
4. Roast in the oven for 15-20 minutes until sweet potatoes are tender and caramelized.
5. In a skillet, heat black beans over medium heat.
6. Mash the beans slightly with a fork and season with salt and pepper.
7. Warm corn or flour tortillas in a dry skillet or microwave.
8. Divide roasted sweet potatoes and black beans evenly among the tortillas.
9. Top with diced avocado, salsa, shredded cabbage or lettuce, and a squeeze of lime juice.
10. Fold or roll up tortillas and serve immediately.
    Nutritional Info (per serving): Calories: 320 | Fat: 8g | Carbs: 55g | Protein: 10g
    Student Vegetarian Function: Flavorful and nutritious tacos featuring black beans and roasted sweet potatoes.

CHICKPEA SALAD SANDWICH

Prep: 10 mins | Serves: 2

INGREDIENTS:

- 1 can (15 oz) chickpeas, drained and rinsed
- 2 tablespoons Greek yogurt or vegan mayonnaise
- 1 tablespoon Dijon mustard
- 1 stalk celery, finely chopped
- 2 tablespoons chopped red onion
- 1 tablespoon chopped fresh dill (or use dried)
- Salt and pepper, to taste
- 4 slices whole grain bread
- Lettuce leaves and sliced tomato (optional)

INSTRUCTIONS:

1. In a mixing bowl, mash chickpeas with a fork or potato masher.
2. Add Greek yogurt or vegan mayonnaise, Dijon mustard, chopped celery, chopped red onion, chopped dill, salt, and pepper.
3. Mix until well combined and creamy.
4. Toast whole grain bread slices if desired.
5. Spread chickpea salad evenly on one side of each bread slice.
6. Top with lettuce leaves and sliced tomato if using.
7. Place the remaining bread slices on top to form sandwiches.
8. Slice in half diagonally and serve immediately.
   Nutritional Info (per serving): Calories: 300 | Fat: 7g | Carbs: 50g | Protein: 15g
   Student Vegetarian Function: A delicious and protein-packed chickpea salad sandwich, perfect for a quick and satisfying meal.

PASTA, NOODLES AND CASSEROLES

EASY VEGETABLE LASAGNA

Prep: 20 mins | Cook: 45 mins | Serves: 6

INGREDIENTS:

- 9 lasagna noodles
- 2 cups marinara sauce
- 1 zucchini, sliced
- 1 yellow squash, sliced
- 1 red bell pepper, sliced
- 1 cup ricotta cheese
- 1 cup shredded mozzarella cheese
- 1/4 cup grated Parmesan cheese
- Salt and pepper, to taste
- Fresh basil leaves, for garnish

INSTRUCTIONS:

1. Preheat oven to 375°F (190°C).
2. Cook lasagna noodles according to package instructions. Drain and set aside.
3. In a baking dish, spread a thin layer of marinara sauce.
4. Layer cooked lasagna noodles, sliced zucchini, yellow squash, and red bell pepper.
5. Dollop ricotta cheese over the vegetables and spread evenly.
6. Sprinkle shredded mozzarella cheese and grated Parmesan cheese on top.
7. Repeat layers, ending with a layer of marinara sauce and cheese.
8. Cover with foil and bake for 30 minutes.
9. Remove foil and bake for an additional 15 minutes until bubbly and golden.
10. Let it cool for 10 minutes before slicing.
11. Garnish with fresh basil leaves before serving.
    Nutritional Info (per serving): Calories: 320 | Fat: 15g | Carbs: 30g | Protein: 18g
    Student Vegetarian Function: One-dish vegetarian comfort food perfect for feeding a crowd.

CREAMY MAC AND CHEESE

Prep: 10 mins | Cook: 20 mins | Serves: 4

INGREDIENTS:

- 8 oz (225g) macaroni or pasta of choice
- 2 tablespoons butter
- 2 tablespoons all-purpose flour
- 2 cups milk
- 2 cups shredded cheddar cheese
- Salt and pepper, to taste
- Optional add-ins: steamed broccoli, diced tomatoes, cooked peas

INSTRUCTIONS:

1. Cook macaroni according to package instructions. Drain and set aside.
2. In a saucepan, melt butter over medium heat.
3. Whisk in flour and cook for 1-2 minutes until golden.
4. Gradually whisk in milk and bring to a simmer.
5. Stir in shredded cheddar cheese until melted and smooth.
6. Season with salt and pepper.
7. Add cooked macaroni to the cheese sauce and stir until well coated.
8. If desired, mix in steamed broccoli, diced tomatoes, or cooked peas.
9. Serve hot and enjoy the creamy goodness!
   Nutritional Info (per serving): Calories: 450 | Fat: 20g | Carbs: 45g | Protein: 20g
   Student Vegetarian Function: Classic comfort food made easy with a creamy cheese sauce.

VEGGIE LO MEIN

Prep: 15 mins | Cook: 10 mins | Serves: 4

INGREDIENTS:

- 8 oz (225g) spaghetti noodles
- 2 tablespoons soy sauce
- 2 tablespoons hoisin sauce
- 1 tablespoon sesame oil
- 1 tablespoon vegetable oil
- 2 cloves garlic, minced
- 1 bell pepper, thinly sliced
- 1 cup sliced mushrooms
- 1 cup shredded cabbage or coleslaw mix
- 1 carrot, julienned
- Green onions, sliced (for garnish)

INSTRUCTIONS:

1. Cook spaghetti noodles according to package instructions. Drain and set aside.
2. In a small bowl, mix soy sauce, hoisin sauce, and sesame oil. Set aside.
3. Heat vegetable oil in a large skillet or wok over medium-high heat.
4. Add minced garlic, bell pepper, mushrooms, shredded cabbage, and julienned carrot. Stir-fry for 3-4 minutes until vegetables are tender-crisp.
5. Add cooked noodles to the skillet.
6. Pour the sauce mixture over the noodles and vegetables.
7. Toss everything together until well combined and heated through.
8. Serve hot, garnished with sliced green onions.

VEGETABLE PAD THAI

Prep: 15 mins | Cook: 15 mins | Serves: 4

INGREDIENTS:

- 8 oz (225g) rice noodles
- 2 tablespoons tamarind paste
- 3 tablespoons soy sauce
- 2 tablespoons brown sugar
- 1 tablespoon lime juice
- 2 tablespoons vegetable oil
- 1 block (14 oz or 400g) firm tofu, pressed and cubed
- 2 cloves garlic, minced
- 1 red bell pepper, thinly sliced
- 1 carrot, julienned
- 1 cup bean sprouts
- 4 green onions, chopped
- Crushed peanuts, for garnish
- Fresh cilantro, for garnish
- Lime wedges, for serving

INSTRUCTIONS:

1. Cook rice noodles according to package instructions. Drain and set aside.
2. In a small bowl, mix tamarind paste, soy sauce, brown sugar, and lime juice to make the sauce. Set aside.
3. In a large skillet or wok, heat vegetable oil over medium-high heat.
4. Add cubed tofu and stir-fry until golden and crispy. Remove tofu from the skillet and set aside.
5. In the same skillet, add minced garlic and cook for 30 seconds until fragrant.
6. Add sliced bell pepper and julienned carrot. Stir-fry for 2-3 minutes until vegetables are tender-crisp.
7. Push vegetables to one side of the skillet and pour the sauce into the empty space.
8. Add cooked rice noodles to the skillet, tossing to coat with the sauce and vegetables.
9. Stir in bean sprouts, chopped green onions, and cooked tofu.
10. Continue to stir-fry for another 2-3 minutes until everything is heated through.
11. Taste and adjust seasoning with more soy sauce, brown sugar, or lime juice if needed.
12. Serve hot, garnished with crushed peanuts, fresh cilantro, and lime wedges on the side.
    Nutritional Info (per serving): Calories: 400 | Fat: 15g | Carbs: 55g | Protein: 15g
    Student Vegetarian Function: A flavorful and satisfying vegetarian version of a classic Thai dish, perfect for a quick and delicious dinner option.

TOMATO AND HERB PASTA

Prep: 10 mins | Cook: 20 mins | Serves: 4

INGREDIENTS:

- 8 oz (225g) penne or fusilli pasta
- 2 tablespoons olive oil

- 2 cloves garlic, minced
- 1 can (14 oz) diced tomatoes
- 1/4 cup chopped fresh basil
- 1/4 cup chopped fresh parsley
- Salt and pepper, to taste
- Grated Parmesan cheese, for serving

INSTRUCTIONS:

1. Cook pasta according to package instructions. Drain and set aside.
2. In a large skillet, heat olive oil over medium heat.
3. Add minced garlic and sauté for 1 minute until fragrant.
4. Stir in diced tomatoes (with juices) and bring to a simmer.
5. Add chopped basil and parsley. Season with salt and pepper.
6. Simmer for 10-15 minutes until the sauce thickens slightly.
7. Add cooked pasta to the skillet and toss to coat evenly.
8. Serve hot, garnished with grated Parmesan cheese.
   Nutritional Info (per serving): Calories: 300 | Fat: 8g | Carbs: 48g | Protein: 10g
   Student Vegetarian Function: Simple yet flavorful pasta dish using pantry staples and fresh herbs.

CLASSIC PESTO PASTA

Prep: 15 mins | Cook: 10 mins | Serves: 4

INGREDIENTS:

- 8 oz (225g) spaghetti or linguine
- 1/2 cup basil pesto (store-bought or homemade)
- 1 cup cherry tomatoes, halved
- 1/4 cup pine nuts, toasted
- Grated Parmesan cheese, for serving
- Salt and pepper, to taste

INSTRUCTIONS:

1. Cook pasta according to package instructions. Drain and set aside.
2. In a large bowl, toss cooked pasta with basil pesto until evenly coated.
3. Add halved cherry tomatoes and toasted pine nuts.
4. Season with salt and pepper, to taste.
5. Serve hot or cold, garnished with grated Parmesan cheese.
   Nutritional Info (per serving): Calories: 400 | Fat: 22g | Carbs: 40g | Protein: 12g
   Student Vegetarian Function: Quick and delicious pesto pasta that's perfect for busy students.

ROASTED VEGETABLE PASTA

Prep: 15 mins | Cook: 30 mins | Serves: 4

INGREDIENTS:

- 8 oz (225g) penne pasta
- 1 zucchini, diced
- 1 yellow squash, diced
- 1 red bell pepper, diced
- 1 onion, sliced
- 3 tablespoons olive oil
- 2 cloves garlic, minced
- Salt and pepper, to taste
- Grated Parmesan cheese, for serving

INSTRUCTIONS:

1. Preheat oven to 400°F (200°C).
2. Toss diced zucchini, yellow squash, red bell pepper, and sliced onion with olive oil, minced garlic, salt, and pepper.
3. Spread vegetables in a single layer on a baking sheet.
4. Roast in the oven for 20-25 minutes until vegetables are tender and caramelized.
5. Meanwhile, cook penne pasta according to package instructions. Drain and set aside.
6. In a large bowl, toss cooked pasta with roasted vegetables.
7. Serve hot, topped with grated Parmesan cheese.
   Nutritional Info (per serving): Calories: 350 | Fat: 12g | Carbs: 52g | Protein: 10g
   Student Vegetarian Function: A flavorful and colorful pasta dish packed with roasted veggies.

EGGPLANT PARMESAN

Prep: 20 mins | Cook: 30 mins | Serves: 4

INGREDIENTS:

- 1 large eggplant, sliced into rounds
- Salt
- 1 cup breadcrumbs (or panko breadcrumbs)
- 1/2 cup grated Parmesan cheese
- 2 eggs, beaten
- 2 cups marinara sauce
- 1 cup shredded mozzarella cheese
- Fresh basil leaves, for garnish

INSTRUCTIONS:

1. Preheat oven to 375°F (190°C).
2. Place eggplant slices on a baking sheet and sprinkle with salt. Let sit for 10-15 minutes to release moisture.

3. Pat eggplant slices dry with paper towels.
4. In a shallow bowl, combine breadcrumbs and grated Parmesan cheese.
5. Dip each eggplant slice into beaten eggs, then coat with breadcrumb mixture.
6. Place coated eggplant slices back on the baking sheet.
7. Bake in the oven for 20-25 minutes until golden and crispy.
8. In a baking dish, spread a thin layer of marinara sauce.
9. Arrange baked eggplant slices in the dish, overlapping slightly.
10. Top with remaining marinara sauce and shredded mozzarella cheese.
11. Bake for 15 minutes until cheese is melted and bubbly.
12. Let it cool for 5 minutes before serving.
13. Garnish with fresh basil leaves.
    Nutritional Info (per serving): Calories: 320 | Fat: 12g | Carbs: 38g | Protein: 15g
    Student Vegetarian Function: A satisfying and cheesy eggplant parmesan that's perfect for a comforting meal.

VEGETABLE POT PIE

Prep: 20 mins | Cook: 30 mins | Serves: 4

INGREDIENTS:

- 1 sheet of puff pastry, thawed
- 2 tablespoons butter
- 1 onion, diced
- 2 carrots, diced
- 2 celery stalks, diced
- 1 cup frozen peas
- 8 oz (225g) mushrooms, sliced
- 2 tablespoons all-purpose flour
- 1 cup vegetable broth
- 1 cup milk (or non-dairy milk)
- 1 teaspoon dried thyme
- Salt and pepper, to taste

INSTRUCTIONS:

1. Preheat oven to 400°F (200°C).
2. In a skillet, melt butter over medium heat.
3. Add diced onion, carrots, celery, mushrooms, and frozen peas. Sauté until vegetables are softened.
4. Stir in all-purpose flour and cook for 1-2 minutes to form a roux.
5. Gradually pour in vegetable broth and milk, stirring constantly until smooth and thickened.
6. Season with dried thyme, salt, and pepper.
7. Transfer the vegetable mixture to a baking dish.
8. Roll out puff pastry and place it over the baking dish, trimming any excess pastry.
9. Cut a few slits on the pastry to allow steam to escape.
10. Bake for 25-30 minutes until the pastry is golden and the filling is bubbly.
11. Let it cool for a few minutes before serving.

Nutritional Info (per serving): Calories: 400 | Fat: 20g | Carbs: 45g | Protein: 10g
Student Vegetarian Function: A hearty and comforting vegetable pot pie topped with flaky puff pastry.

ENCHILADAS

Prep: 20 mins | Cook: 30 mins | Serves: 4

INGREDIENTS:

- 8 corn tortillas
- 2 cups cooked black beans
- 1 bell pepper, diced
- 1 small onion, diced
- 1 cup enchilada sauce (store-bought or homemade)
- 1 cup shredded cheese (cheddar, Monterey Jack, or Mexican blend)
- Optional toppings: diced avocado, sliced jalapeños, chopped cilantro

INSTRUCTIONS:

1. Preheat oven to 375°F (190°C).
2. In a skillet, sauté diced bell pepper and onion until softened.
3. Add cooked black beans to the skillet and stir to combine.
4. Pour a small amount of enchilada sauce into the bottom of a baking dish.
5. Warm corn tortillas in the microwave or on a skillet to make them pliable.
6. Spoon black bean mixture into each tortilla and roll up.
7. Place rolled tortillas seam-side down in the baking dish.
8. Pour remaining enchilada sauce over the top.
9. Sprinkle shredded cheese evenly over the enchiladas.
10. Cover with foil and bake for 20 minutes.
11. Remove foil and bake for an additional 10 minutes until cheese is melted and bubbly.
12. Serve hot, topped with optional toppings like diced avocado, sliced jalapeños, and chopped cilantro.
    Nutritional Info (per serving): Calories: 380 | Fat: 15g | Carbs: 50g | Protein: 15g
    Student Vegetarian Function: Flavorful and satisfying enchiladas filled with black beans and veggies.

BAKED ZITI

Prep: 15 mins | Cook: 30 mins | Serves: 6

INGREDIENTS:

- 12 oz (340g) ziti or penne pasta
- 2 cups marinara sauce
- 1 cup ricotta cheese
- 1 cup shredded mozzarella cheese
- 1/2 cup grated Parmesan cheese
- 1 teaspoon dried oregano
- Salt and pepper, to taste
- Fresh basil leaves, for garnish

INSTRUCTIONS:

1. Preheat oven to 375°F (190°C).
2. Cook ziti or penne pasta according to package instructions. Drain and set aside.
3. In a large bowl, combine cooked pasta, marinara sauce, ricotta cheese, shredded mozzarella cheese, grated Parmesan cheese, dried oregano, salt, and pepper.
4. Transfer the pasta mixture to a baking dish.
5. Sprinkle additional shredded mozzarella cheese and grated Parmesan cheese on top.
6. Cover with foil and bake for 20 minutes.
7. Remove foil and bake for an additional 10 minutes until cheese is melted and bubbly.
8. Let it cool for a few minutes before serving.
9. Garnish with fresh basil leaves.
   Nutritional Info (per serving): Calories: 450 | Fat: 15g | Carbs: 55g | Protein: 20g
   Student Vegetarian Function: A comforting and cheesy baked pasta dish that's perfect for sharing.

VEGETABLE FRIED RICE

Prep: 15 mins | Cook: 15 mins | Serves: 4

INGREDIENTS:

- 2 cups cooked rice (preferably day-old)
- 2 tablespoons vegetable oil
- 1 onion, diced
- 2 cloves garlic, minced
- 1 carrot, diced
- 1 cup frozen peas
- 2 tablespoons soy sauce
- 1 tablespoon sesame oil
- 2 green onions, sliced (for garnish)
- Optional add-ins: diced bell peppers, broccoli florets, scrambled tofu

INSTRUCTIONS:

1. Heat vegetable oil in a large skillet or wok over medium-high heat.
2. Add diced onion and minced garlic, and sauté until fragrant.
3. Stir in diced carrot and cook for 2-3 minutes until slightly tender.
4. Add cooked rice and frozen peas to the skillet.
5. Drizzle soy sauce and sesame oil over the rice mixture.
6. Stir-fry for 5-7 minutes until everything is heated through and well combined.
7. If using optional add-ins like diced bell peppers or broccoli florets, add them now and cook until tender-crisp.
8. Garnish with sliced green onions before serving.
   Nutritional Info (per serving): Calories: 300 | Fat: 10g | Carbs: 45g | Protein: 8g
   Student Vegetarian Function: Quick and easy vegetable fried rice using simple ingredients and pantry staples.

MUSHROOM STROGANOFF

Prep: 10 mins | Cook: 20 mins | Serves: 4

INGREDIENTS:

- 8 oz (225g) egg noodles or pasta of choice
- 2 tablespoons butter
- 1 onion, diced
- 8 oz (225g) cremini mushrooms, sliced
- 2 cloves garlic, minced
- 2 tablespoons all-purpose flour
- 1 cup vegetable broth
- 1 cup sour cream or Greek yogurt
- 2 tablespoons Dijon mustard
- Salt and pepper, to taste
- Fresh parsley, chopped (for garnish)

INSTRUCTIONS:

1. Cook egg noodles or pasta according to package instructions. Drain and set aside.
2. In a large skillet, melt butter over medium heat.
3. Add diced onion and sliced mushrooms. Sauté until mushrooms release their liquid and start to brown.
4. Stir in minced garlic and cook for 1 minute.
5. Sprinkle all-purpose flour over the mushroom mixture and stir to coat.
6. Gradually pour in vegetable broth, stirring constantly to avoid lumps.
7. Add sour cream (or Greek yogurt) and Dijon mustard. Stir until well combined.
8. Simmer for 5-7 minutes until the sauce thickens.
9. Season with salt and pepper, to taste.
10. Add cooked noodles to the skillet and toss to coat in the creamy mushroom sauce.
11. Garnish with chopped fresh parsley before serving.
    Nutritional Info (per serving): Calories: 400 | Fat: 18g | Carbs: 48g | Protein: 12g
    Student Vegetarian Function: A comforting and creamy mushroom stroganoff that's ready in no time.

VEGGIE SHEPHERD'S PIE

Prep: 20 mins | Cook: 30 mins | Serves: 4

INGREDIENTS:

- 2 large potatoes, peeled and diced
- Salt
- 2 tablespoons butter
- 1 onion, diced
- 2 carrots, diced
- 1 cup frozen peas
- 8 oz (225g) mushrooms, sliced
- 1 tablespoon tomato paste

- 1 cup vegetable broth
- 1 tablespoon Worcestershire sauce (vegetarian-friendly)
- 1 teaspoon dried thyme
- Salt and pepper, to taste
- Grated cheddar cheese, for topping (optional)

INSTRUCTIONS:

1. Preheat oven to 375°F (190°C).
2. Place diced potatoes in a pot of salted water. Bring to a boil and cook until potatoes are tender. Drain and mash with butter. Season with salt. Set aside.
3. In a skillet, heat olive oil over medium heat.
4. Add diced onion, carrots, and mushrooms. Sauté until vegetables are softened.
5. Stir in tomato paste, vegetable broth, Worcestershire sauce, dried thyme, salt, and pepper.
6. Add frozen peas and cook for 2-3 minutes until heated through.
7. Transfer vegetable mixture to a baking dish.
8. Spread mashed potatoes over the top, covering the vegetables.
9. If desired, sprinkle grated cheddar cheese on top.
10. Bake for 20-25 minutes until bubbly and golden.
11. Let it cool for 5 minutes before serving.
    Nutritional Info (per serving): Calories: 350 | Fat: 10g | Carbs: 55g | Protein: 10g
    Student Vegetarian Function: A hearty and satisfying veggie shepherd's pie, perfect for a comforting dinner.

CURRIES, STIR FRIES AND ONE POTS

CHICKPEA CURRY

Prep: 10 mins | Cook: 20 mins | Serves: 4

INGREDIENTS:

- 1 tablespoon vegetable oil
- 1 onion, diced
- 3 cloves garlic, minced
- 1 tablespoon grated ginger
- 1 tablespoon curry powder
- 1 teaspoon ground cumin
- 1 teaspoon ground coriander
- 1 can (15 oz) chickpeas, drained and rinsed
- 1 can (14 oz) diced tomatoes
- 1 can (14 oz) coconut milk
- Salt and pepper, to taste
- Fresh cilantro, for garnish

INSTRUCTIONS:

1. Heat vegetable oil in a large skillet over medium heat.
2. Add diced onion, minced garlic, and grated ginger. Sauté until onion is soft and translucent.
3. Stir in curry powder, ground cumin, and ground coriander. Cook for 1 minute until fragrant.
4. Add drained chickpeas, diced tomatoes, and coconut milk to the skillet.
5. Simmer for 10-15 minutes until the sauce thickens slightly.
6. Season with salt and pepper to taste.
7. Garnish with fresh cilantro before serving.
   Nutritional Info (per serving): Calories: 320 | Fat: 18g | Carbs: 30g | Protein: 8g
   Student Vegetarian Function: Quick and flavorful chickpea curry for a satisfying meal.

LENTIL CURRY

Prep: 10 mins | Cook: 30 mins | Serves: 4

INGREDIENTS:

- 1 tablespoon vegetable oil
- 1 onion, diced
- 2 carrots, diced
- 3 cloves garlic, minced
- 1 tablespoon grated ginger
- 1 tablespoon curry powder
- 1 teaspoon ground turmeric
- 1 cup dried lentils, rinsed
- 3 cups vegetable broth

- 1 can (14 oz) coconut milk
- Salt and pepper, to taste
- Fresh cilantro, for garnish

INSTRUCTIONS:

1. Heat vegetable oil in a large pot over medium heat.
2. Add diced onion and carrots. Sauté until vegetables start to soften.
3. Stir in minced garlic, grated ginger, curry powder, and ground turmeric. Cook for 1 minute until fragrant.
4. Add rinsed lentils and vegetable broth to the pot.
5. Bring to a boil, then reduce heat and simmer for 20-25 minutes until lentils are tender.
6. Stir in coconut milk and simmer for another 5 minutes.
7. Season with salt and pepper to taste.
8. Garnish with fresh cilantro before serving.
   Nutritional Info (per serving): Calories: 380 | Fat: 18g | Carbs: 42g | Protein: 15g
   Student Vegetarian Function: Hearty lentil curry packed with protein and fiber.

VEGETABLE COCONUT CURRY

Prep: 15 mins | Cook: 20 mins | Serves: 4

INGREDIENTS:

- 1 tablespoon vegetable oil
- 1 onion, diced
- 2 bell peppers, diced
- 1 zucchini, diced
- 1 cup broccoli florets
- 3 tablespoons red curry paste
- 1 can (14 oz) coconut milk
- 1 tablespoon soy sauce
- 1 tablespoon brown sugar
- Salt, to taste
- Fresh basil or cilantro, for garnish

INSTRUCTIONS:

1. Heat vegetable oil in a large skillet or wok over medium-high heat.
2. Add diced onion and bell peppers. Sauté until vegetables start to soften.
3. Stir in diced zucchini and broccoli florets.
4. Add red curry paste to the vegetables and cook for 1 minute.
5. Pour in coconut milk, soy sauce, and brown sugar. Stir to combine.
6. Simmer for 10-12 minutes until vegetables are tender.
7. Season with salt to taste.
8. Garnish with fresh basil or cilantro before serving.
   Nutritional Info (per serving): Calories: 280 | Fat: 20g | Carbs: 22g | Protein: 6g
   Student Vegetarian Function: Creamy and aromatic vegetable coconut curry for a delightful dinner.

TOFU TIKKA MASALA

Prep: 15 mins | Cook: 25 mins | Serves: 4

INGREDIENTS:

- 1 block (14 oz or 400g) firm tofu, pressed and cubed
- 2 tablespoons vegetable oil
- 1 onion, diced
- 3 cloves garlic, minced
- 1 tablespoon grated ginger
- 2 tablespoons tikka masala spice blend
- 1 can (14 oz) diced tomatoes
- 1 cup vegetable broth
- 1/2 cup heavy cream or coconut cream
- Salt and pepper, to taste
- Fresh cilantro, for garnish

INSTRUCTIONS:

1. Heat vegetable oil in a large skillet over medium heat.
2. Add cubed tofu and cook until golden and crispy on all sides. Remove tofu from the skillet and set aside.
3. In the same skillet, add diced onion and sauté until translucent.
4. Stir in minced garlic, grated ginger, and tikka masala spice blend. Cook for 1 minute until fragrant.
5. Add diced tomatoes and vegetable broth to the skillet.
6. Simmer for 10-12 minutes until the sauce thickens.
7. Stir in heavy cream or coconut cream and cooked tofu.
8. Simmer for another 5 minutes.
9. Season with salt and pepper to taste.
10. Garnish with fresh cilantro before serving.
    Nutritional Info (per serving): Calories: 380 | Fat: 28g | Carbs: 16g | Protein: 18g
    Student Vegetarian Function: Flavorful tofu tikka masala for a satisfying Indian-inspired meal.

SWEET POTATO CHICKPEA BUDDHA BOWL

Prep: 15 mins | Cook: 25 mins | Serves: 4

INGREDIENTS:

- 2 sweet potatoes, peeled and diced
- 1 can (15 oz) chickpeas, drained and rinsed
- 2 tablespoons olive oil
- 1 teaspoon smoked paprika
- Salt and pepper, to taste
- 4 cups cooked quinoa or brown rice
- 2 cups baby spinach or kale
- 1 avocado, sliced
- Tahini dressing or lemon tahini sauce, for drizzling

INSTRUCTIONS:

1. Preheat oven to 400°F (200°C).
2. Toss diced sweet potatoes and chickpeas with olive oil, smoked paprika, salt, and pepper.
3. Spread sweet potatoes and chickpeas on a baking sheet in a single layer.
4. Roast in the oven for 20-25 minutes until sweet potatoes are tender.
5. Divide cooked quinoa or brown rice among serving bowls.
6. Top with roasted sweet potatoes, chickpeas, baby spinach or kale, and sliced avocado.
7. Drizzle with tahini dressing or lemon tahini sauce.
8. Serve immediately.

    Nutritional Info (per serving): Calories: 420 | Fat: 18g | Carbs: 55g | Protein: 12g

    Student Vegetarian Function: Nutrient-packed Buddha bowl with sweet potatoes, chickpeas, and greens.

VEGGIE STIR FRY 3 WAYS

Prep: 10 mins | Cook: 10 mins | Serves: 4

INGREDIENTS:

- Stir Fry Base:
- 1 tablespoon vegetable oil
- 1 onion, sliced
- 2 bell peppers, sliced
- 1 cup broccoli florets
- 1 carrot, julienned
- 2 cloves garlic, minced
- 1-inch piece ginger, grated
- Soy sauce, to taste

VARIATIONS:

1. Teriyaki Stir Fry:

    2 tablespoons teriyaki sauce

    1 tablespoon sesame seeds, for garnish

2. Spicy Szechuan Stir Fry:

    2 tablespoons Szechuan sauce

    Crushed red pepper flakes, to taste

    Green onions, sliced, for garnish

3. Garlic Ginger Stir Fry:

    2 tablespoons hoisin sauce

    1 tablespoon rice vinegar

    Fresh cilantro, chopped, for garnish

INSTRUCTIONS:

1. Heat vegetable oil in a large skillet or wok over high heat.
2. Add sliced onion, bell peppers, broccoli florets, julienned carrot, minced garlic, and grated ginger to the skillet.
3. Stir fry for 5-6 minutes until vegetables are tender-crisp.
4. Divide the stir-fried vegetables into three portions in separate bowls.
5. For each variation: Add the respective sauce (teriyaki, Szechuan, or hoisin) to the portioned vegetables and toss to coat.
6. Serve each variation of stir fry over cooked rice or noodles.
7. Garnish with sesame seeds, crushed red pepper flakes, green onions, or fresh cilantro as desired.
   Nutritional Info (per serving for base stir fry): Calories: 120 | Fat: 5g | Carbs: 15g | Protein: 3g
   Student Vegetarian Function: Versatile veggie stir fry with three delicious flavor variations.

FRIED RICE 3 WAYS

Prep: 10 mins | Cook: 10 mins | Serves: 4

INGREDIENTS:

- Fried Rice Base:
- 2 cups cooked rice (preferably day-old)
- 2 tablespoons soy sauce
- 1 tablespoon vegetable oil
- 1 onion, diced
- 1 cup mixed vegetables (peas, carrots, corn)
- 2 cloves garlic, minced
- 2 eggs, beaten (optional for vegetarian version)

VARIATIONS:

1. Classic Vegetable Fried Rice:

   Additional soy sauce, to taste

   Green onions, chopped, for garnish

2. Pineapple Fried Rice:

   1 cup diced pineapple

   2 tablespoons sweet chili sauce

   Cashew nuts, for garnish

3. Spicy Kimchi Fried Rice:

   1 cup kimchi, chopped

   1 tablespoon gochujang (Korean chili paste)

   Sesame seeds, for garnish

INSTRUCTIONS:

1. Heat vegetable oil in a large skillet or wok over medium-high heat.
2. Add diced onion and mixed vegetables to the skillet. Stir fry for 3-4 minutes until vegetables are tender.
3. Push vegetables to one side of the skillet and pour beaten eggs into the empty space. Scramble the eggs until cooked through.
4. Mix the scrambled eggs with the vegetables.
5. Add cooked rice and soy sauce to the skillet. Stir fry for 3-4 minutes until rice is heated through.
6. Divide the fried rice into three portions in separate bowls.
7. For each variation: Add the respective ingredients (pineapple with sweet chili sauce, kimchi with gochujang, or additional soy sauce for classic) to the portioned fried rice and toss to combine.
8. Garnish each variation with chopped green onions, cashew nuts, or sesame seeds as desired.
   Nutritional Info (per serving for base fried rice): Calories: 220 | Fat: 8g | Carbs: 30g | Protein: 6g
   Student Vegetarian Function: Quick and customizable fried rice with three unique flavor twists.

CHILI SIN CARNE

Prep: 15 mins | Cook: 30 mins | Serves: 6

INGREDIENTS:

- 1 tablespoon vegetable oil
- 1 onion, diced
- 2 bell peppers, diced
- 3 cloves garlic, minced
- 1 tablespoon chili powder
- 1 teaspoon ground cumin
- 1 can (15 oz) kidney beans, drained and rinsed
- 1 can (15 oz) black beans, drained and rinsed
- 1 can (14 oz) diced tomatoes
- 1 cup vegetable broth
- Salt and pepper, to taste
- Optional toppings: diced avocado, chopped cilantro, shredded cheese, sour cream

INSTRUCTIONS:

1. Heat vegetable oil in a large pot over medium heat.
2. Add diced onion and bell peppers. Sauté for 5 minutes until vegetables start to soften.
3. Stir in minced garlic, chili powder, and ground cumin. Cook for 1 minute until fragrant.
4. Add kidney beans, black beans, diced tomatoes, and vegetable broth to the pot.
5. Bring to a boil, then reduce heat and simmer for 20-25 minutes.
6. Season with salt and pepper to taste.
7. Serve hot, topped with diced avocado, chopped cilantro, shredded cheese, or sour cream as desired.
   Nutritional Info (per serving): Calories: 250 | Fat: 5g | Carbs: 40g | Protein: 12g
   Student Vegetarian Function: Hearty and satisfying chili sin carne, perfect for a comforting meal.

RATATOUILLE

Prep: 15 mins | Cook: 30 mins | Serves: 4

INGREDIENTS:

- 2 tablespoons olive oil
- 1 onion, sliced
- 2 cloves garlic, minced
- 1 eggplant, diced
- 2 zucchinis, sliced
- 1 bell pepper, diced
- 1 can (14 oz) diced tomatoes
- 1 tablespoon tomato paste
- 1 teaspoon dried thyme
- Salt and pepper, to taste
- Fresh basil, chopped, for garnish

INSTRUCTIONS:

1. Heat olive oil in a large skillet or pot over medium heat.
2. Add sliced onion and minced garlic. Sauté until onion is soft and translucent.
3. Add diced eggplant, sliced zucchini, and diced bell pepper to the skillet. Cook for 5-7 minutes until vegetables start to soften.
4. Stir in diced tomatoes, tomato paste, and dried thyme.
5. Season with salt and pepper to taste.
6. Simmer for 15-20 minutes until vegetables are tender and the sauce has thickened.
7. Garnish with fresh chopped basil before serving.
   Nutritional Info (per serving): Calories: 180 | Fat: 7g | Carbs: 28g | Protein: 5g
   Student Vegetarian Function: Flavorful and colorful ratatouille with a mix of seasonal vegetables.

BIBIMBAP

Prep: 20 mins | Cook: 20 mins | Serves: 4

INGREDIENTS:

- 2 cups cooked rice (white or brown)
- 1 block (14 oz or 400g) firm tofu, pressed and sliced
- 2 tablespoons soy sauce
- 1 tablespoon sesame oil
- 1 tablespoon vegetable oil
- 1 carrot, julienned
- 1 zucchini, julienned
- 1 cup spinach
- 4 shiitake mushrooms, sliced
- 1 tablespoon gochujang (Korean chili paste)
- 2 green onions, chopped

- Sesame seeds, for garnish

INSTRUCTIONS:

1. Cook rice according to package instructions and set aside.
2. Marinate sliced tofu in soy sauce and sesame oil for 10 minutes.
3. Heat vegetable oil in a skillet over medium heat. Add marinated tofu and cook until golden and crispy on both sides. Remove from skillet and set aside.
4. In the same skillet, stir fry julienned carrot, zucchini, spinach, and shiitake mushrooms until tender.
5. To assemble, divide cooked rice among serving bowls. Arrange cooked vegetables and tofu on top of the rice.
6. Place a dollop of gochujang in the center.
7. Garnish with chopped green onions and sesame seeds.
8. Mix everything together before eating.
   Nutritional Info (per serving): Calories: 350 | Fat: 14g | Carbs: 42g | Protein: 15g
   Student Vegetarian Function: Bibimbap is a customizable and nutritious Korean rice bowl.

CAULIFLOWER TACO BOWL

Prep: 15 mins | Cook: 25 mins | Serves: 4

INGREDIENTS:

- 1 head cauliflower, cut into florets
- 1 tablespoon chili powder
- 1 teaspoon ground cumin
- 1 teaspoon smoked paprika
- Salt and pepper, to taste
- 1 tablespoon vegetable oil
- 1 can (15 oz) black beans, drained and rinsed
- 1 cup corn kernels (fresh or frozen)
- 1 cup cooked quinoa or rice
- Salsa, guacamole, and sour cream, for serving

INSTRUCTIONS:

1. Preheat oven to 400°F (200°C).
2. Toss cauliflower florets with chili powder, ground cumin, smoked paprika, salt, pepper, and vegetable oil on a baking sheet.
3. Roast in the oven for 20-25 minutes until cauliflower is tender and slightly browned.
4. In a skillet, heat black beans and corn kernels until heated through.
5. To assemble taco bowls, divide cooked quinoa or rice among serving bowls.
6. Top with roasted cauliflower, black beans, corn, salsa, guacamole, and sour cream.
7. Serve hot.
   Nutritional Info (per serving): Calories: 280 | Fat: 8g | Carbs: 45g | Protein: 10g
   Student Vegetarian Function: Cauliflower taco bowl is a satisfying and veggie-packed meal inspired by Mexican flavors.

QUINOA STUFFED PEPPERS

Prep: 20 mins | Cook: 30 mins | Serves: 4

INGREDIENTS:

- 4 bell peppers, tops cut off and seeds removed
- 1 cup quinoa, cooked
- 1 can (15 oz) black beans, drained and rinsed
- 1 cup corn kernels (fresh or frozen)
- 1 cup diced tomatoes
- 1 teaspoon chili powder
- 1 teaspoon ground cumin
- Salt and pepper, to taste
- Grated cheese, for topping (optional)

INSTRUCTIONS:

1. Preheat oven to 375°F (190°C).
2. In a bowl, mix cooked quinoa, black beans, corn kernels, diced tomatoes, chili powder, ground cumin, salt, and pepper.
3. Stuff each bell pepper with the quinoa mixture.
4. Place stuffed peppers in a baking dish.
5. Cover with foil and bake for 25-30 minutes until peppers are tender.
6. If using cheese, remove foil and sprinkle grated cheese over the stuffed peppers. Bake for an additional 5 minutes until cheese is melted.
7. Serve hot.
   Nutritional Info (per serving): Calories: 320 | Fat: 5g | Carbs: 60g | Protein: 14g
   Student Vegetarian Function: Quinoa stuffed peppers are a wholesome and colorful meal that's easy to prepare.

CHANA MASALA

Prep: 15 mins | Cook: 25 mins | Serves: 4

INGREDIENTS:

- 2 tablespoons vegetable oil
- 1 onion, finely chopped
- 3 cloves garlic, minced
- 1 tablespoon grated ginger
- 1 green chili, finely chopped (optional)
- 1 tablespoon ground coriander
- 1 teaspoon ground cumin
- 1/2 teaspoon turmeric powder
- 1/2 teaspoon paprika
- 1 can (15 oz) chickpeas, drained and rinsed
- 1 can (14 oz) diced tomatoes

- Salt, to taste
- Fresh cilantro, chopped, for garnish

INSTRUCTIONS:

1. Heat vegetable oil in a skillet over medium heat.
2. Add finely chopped onion and sauté until translucent.
3. Stir in minced garlic, grated ginger, and chopped green chili. Cook for 1 minute until fragrant.
4. Add ground coriander, ground cumin, turmeric powder, and paprika. Cook for another minute.
5. Add drained chickpeas and diced tomatoes to the skillet. Stir to combine.
6. Simmer for 15-20 minutes until the sauce thickens.
7. Season with salt to taste.
8. Garnish with chopped fresh cilantro before serving.
   Nutritional Info (per serving): Calories: 240 | Fat: 8g | Carbs: 34g | Protein: 8g
   Student Vegetarian Function: Chana masala is a flavorful Indian chickpea curry that pairs well with rice or naan.

DAL MAKHANI

Prep: 15 mins | Cook: 1 hour | Serves: 4

INGREDIENTS:

- 1 cup whole black lentils (urad dal), soaked overnight
- 1/4 cup red kidney beans (rajma), soaked overnight
- 2 tablespoons butter or ghee
- 1 onion, finely chopped
- 3 cloves garlic, minced
- 1 tablespoon grated ginger
- 2 tomatoes, pureed
- 1 teaspoon cumin seeds
- 1 teaspoon garam masala
- 1/2 teaspoon turmeric powder
- 1/2 teaspoon red chili powder (optional)
- Salt, to taste
- 1/4 cup cream (or coconut cream for vegan version)
- Fresh cilantro, chopped, for garnish

INSTRUCTIONS:

1. Drain soaked lentils and kidney beans. In a large pot, combine lentils, kidney beans, and enough water to cover. Bring to a boil, then reduce heat and simmer until lentils are tender (about 30-40 minutes).
2. In a separate skillet, heat butter or ghee over medium heat.
3. Add finely chopped onion and sauté until golden brown.
4. Stir in minced garlic and grated ginger. Cook for 1 minute until fragrant.
5. Add pureed tomatoes, cumin seeds, garam masala, turmeric powder, and red chili powder (if using) to the skillet. Cook for 5-7 minutes until the mixture thickens.

6. Add the cooked lentils and kidney beans (along with some of the cooking liquid) to the skillet. Stir to combine.
7. Simmer for another 15-20 minutes, stirring occasionally.
8. Stir in cream (or coconut cream) and season with salt to taste.
9. Garnish with chopped fresh cilantro before serving.

   Nutritional Info (per serving): Calories: 350 | Fat: 10g | Carbs: 48g | Protein: 15g

   Student Vegetarian Function: Dal makhani is a rich and creamy lentil dish that's perfect with naan or rice.

BEANS AND LENTILS

BEANS AND RICE

Prep: 10 mins | Cook: 30 mins | Serves: 4

INGREDIENTS:

- 1 cup long-grain white rice (200g)
- 1 tablespoon vegetable oil
- 1 onion, diced
- 2 cloves garlic, minced
- 1 bell pepper, diced
- 1 can (15 oz) red kidney beans, drained and rinsed
- 1 teaspoon smoked paprika
- 1 teaspoon dried thyme
- Salt and pepper, to taste
- Chopped green onions, for garnish

INSTRUCTIONS:

1. Cook the white rice according to package instructions.
2. Heat vegetable oil in a skillet over medium heat.
3. Add diced onion, minced garlic, and diced bell pepper. Sauté for 5 minutes until vegetables are softened.
4. Stir in red kidney beans, smoked paprika, dried thyme, salt, and pepper. Cook for another 5 minutes until heated through.
5. Serve the bean mixture over cooked rice.
6. Garnish with chopped green onions before serving.
   Nutritional Info (per serving): Calories: 320 | Fat: 4g | Carbs: 62g | Protein: 11g
   Student Vegetarian Function: Quick and flavorful red beans and rice, perfect for a satisfying meal.

BLACK BEAN BURGERS

Prep: 15 mins | Cook: 15 mins | Serves: 4

INGREDIENTS:

- 1 can (15 oz) black beans, drained and rinsed
- 1/2 cup breadcrumbs (60g)
- 1 egg (or flaxseed meal for vegan version)
- 1/2 bell pepper, finely diced
- 1/4 cup chopped cilantro
- 1 teaspoon cumin
- 1 teaspoon chili powder
- Salt and pepper, to taste
- Burger buns and toppings of choice

INSTRUCTIONS:

1. In a mixing bowl, mash black beans with a fork or potato masher.
2. Add breadcrumbs, egg (or flaxseed meal), diced bell pepper, chopped cilantro, cumin, chili powder, salt, and pepper. Mix until well combined.
3. Divide the mixture into 4 portions and shape into burger patties.
4. Heat a skillet or grill pan over medium heat. Cook the burger patties for 3-4 minutes on each side until golden and cooked through.
5. Serve the black bean burgers on burger buns with your favorite toppings.
   Nutritional Info (per serving without bun and toppings): Calories: 220 | Fat: 3g | Carbs: 38g | Protein: 13g
   Student Vegetarian Function: Homemade black bean burgers that are hearty and packed with flavor.

LENTIL MEATBALLS 4 WAYS

Prep: 15 mins | Cook: 25 mins | Serves: 4

INGREDIENTS:

- 1 cup cooked lentils (200g)
- 1/2 cup breadcrumbs (60g)
- 1/4 cup grated Parmesan cheese (or nutritional yeast for vegan version)
- 1 egg (or flaxseed meal for vegan version)
- 2 tablespoons chopped fresh parsley
- Salt and pepper, to taste
- Olive oil, for cooking

VARIATIONS:

1. Classic Marinara Meatballs:

   Marinara sauce, for serving

   Cooked spaghetti, for serving

2. Sweet and Sour Meatballs:

   Sweet and sour sauce, for serving

   Steamed rice or noodles, for serving

3. Barbecue Meatballs:

   Barbecue sauce, for serving

   Mashed potatoes, for serving

4. Creamy Mushroom Meatballs:

   Creamy mushroom sauce, for serving

   Mashed potatoes or pasta, for serving

INSTRUCTIONS:

1. In a mixing bowl, combine cooked lentils, breadcrumbs, grated Parmesan cheese, egg, chopped fresh parsley, salt, and pepper. Mix until well combined.
2. Divide the mixture into small portions and shape into meatballs.
3. Heat olive oil in a skillet over medium heat.
4. Cook the lentil meatballs in the skillet, turning occasionally, until golden and cooked through (about 10-12 minutes).
5. Serve the lentil meatballs with your choice of sauce and side dishes for each variation.
   Nutritional Info (per serving without sauce and sides): Calories: 220 | Fat: 7g | Carbs. 20g | Protein: 12g
   Student Vegetarian Function: Versatile lentil meatballs that can be enjoyed in different ways with various sauces.

LENTIL BOLOGNESE

Prep: 10 mins | Cook: 25 mins | Serves: 4

INGREDIENTS:

- 1 cup cooked lentils (200g)
- 1 tablespoon olive oil
- 1 onion, diced
- 2 cloves garlic, minced
- 1 carrot, grated
- 1 celery stalk, diced
- 1 can (14 oz) crushed tomatoes
- 1 tablespoon tomato paste
- 1 teaspoon dried oregano
- Salt and pepper, to taste
- Cooked spaghetti or pasta, for serving
- Grated Parmesan cheese (optional), for serving

INSTRUCTIONS:

1. Heat olive oil in a skillet over medium heat.
2. Add diced onion and minced garlic. Sauté for 3-4 minutes until onion is translucent.
3. Stir in grated carrot and diced celery. Cook for another 3-4 minutes until vegetables are softened.
4. Add cooked lentils, crushed tomatoes, tomato paste, dried oregano, salt, and pepper to the skillet. Stir to combine.
5. Simmer the lentil Bolognese sauce for 15-20 minutes, stirring occasionally.
6. Serve the lentil Bolognese over cooked spaghetti or pasta.
7. Garnish with grated Parmesan cheese, if desired.
   Nutritional Info (per serving without pasta and cheese): Calories: 180 | Fat: 4g | Carbs: 28g | Protein: 9g
   Student Vegetarian Function: Lentil Bolognese is a hearty and nutritious alternative to traditional meat sauce.

MUJADDARA

Prep: 10 mins | Cook: 40 mins | Serves: 4

INGREDIENTS:

- 1 cup brown or green lentils, rinsed
- 1/2 cup long-grain rice
- 2 large onions, thinly sliced
- 4 tablespoons olive oil
- 1 teaspoon cumin powder
- Salt and pepper, to taste
- Yogurt (optional), for serving
- Fresh parsley, chopped, for garnish

INSTRUCTIONS:

1. In a saucepan, combine lentils and rice with 3 cups of water. Bring to a boil, then reduce heat and simmer for 20-25 minutes until both are cooked and water is absorbed.
2. While lentils and rice are cooking, heat olive oil in a skillet over medium heat.
3. Add thinly sliced onions and cook slowly, stirring occasionally, until caramelized and golden brown (about 20-25 minutes).
4. Season the onions with cumin powder, salt, and pepper.
5. To serve, spread the cooked lentils and rice on a serving platter.
6. Top with caramelized onions.
7. Serve with yogurt on the side and garnish with chopped fresh parsley.
   Nutritional Info (per serving): Calories: 380 | Fat: 15g | Carbs: 50g | Protein: 13g
   Student Vegetarian Function: Mujaddara is a comforting Middle Eastern dish made with lentils, rice, and caramelized onions.

RED LENTIL CURRY

Prep: 10 mins | Cook: 25 mins | Serves: 4

INGREDIENTS:

- 1 cup red lentils, rinsed
- 1 onion, finely chopped
- 3 cloves garlic, minced
- 1 tablespoon grated ginger
- 1 tablespoon curry powder
- 1 can (14 oz) coconut milk
- 1 can (14 oz) diced tomatoes
- 2 cups vegetable broth
- Salt and pepper, to taste
- Fresh cilantro, chopped, for garnish

INSTRUCTIONS:

1. In a large pot or skillet, sauté chopped onion, minced garlic, and grated ginger until softened.
2. Stir in curry powder and cook for another minute until fragrant.
3. Add red lentils, coconut milk, diced tomatoes, and vegetable broth to the pot. Season with salt and pepper.
4. Bring to a boil, then reduce heat and simmer for 20-25 minutes until lentils are cooked and curry has thickened.
5. Adjust seasoning if needed.
6. Serve the red lentil curry hot, garnished with chopped fresh cilantro.
   Nutritional Info (per serving): Calories: 320 | Fat: 15g | Carbs: 35g | Protein: 15g
   Student Vegetarian Function: Red lentil curry is a quick and flavorful dish that's perfect for busy students.

CHICKPEA TOMATO STEW

Prep: 10 mins | Cook: 25 mins | Serves: 4

INGREDIENTS:

- 2 tablespoons olive oil
- 1 onion, diced
- 3 cloves garlic, minced
- 1 teaspoon ground cumin
- 1 teaspoon smoked paprika
- 1 can (15 oz) chickpeas, drained and rinsed
- 1 can (14 oz) diced tomatoes
- 1 cup vegetable broth
- Salt and pepper, to taste
- Fresh parsley, chopped, for garnish

INSTRUCTIONS:

1. Heat olive oil in a skillet over medium heat.
2. Add diced onion and minced garlic. Sauté until onion is translucent.
3. Stir in ground cumin and smoked paprika. Cook for another minute until fragrant.
4. Add chickpeas, diced tomatoes, and vegetable broth to the skillet. Season with salt and pepper.
5. Simmer for 15-20 minutes until the stew has thickened slightly.
6. Adjust seasoning if needed.
7. Serve the chickpea tomato stew hot, garnished with chopped fresh parsley.
   Nutritional Info (per serving): Calories: 260 | Fat: 10g | Carbs: 35g | Protein: 10g
   Student Vegetarian Function: Chickpea tomato stew is a hearty and satisfying meal that's full of flavor.

WHITE BEAN AND KALE SOUP

Prep: 10 mins | Cook: 25 mins | Serves: 4

INGREDIENTS:

- 2 tablespoons olive oil
- 1 onion, diced
- 3 cloves garlic, minced
- 1 carrot, diced
- 1 celery stalk, diced
- 1 can (15 oz) white beans, drained and rinsed
- 4 cups vegetable broth
- 1 bunch kale, stems removed and leaves chopped
- Salt and pepper, to taste
- Grated Parmesan cheese (optional), for serving

INSTRUCTIONS:

1. Heat olive oil in a large pot over medium heat.
2. Add diced onion, minced garlic, diced carrot, and diced celery. Sauté until vegetables are softened.
3. Stir in white beans and vegetable broth. Bring to a boil.
4. Reduce heat and simmer for 15 minutes.
5. Add chopped kale to the pot and cook for another 5-7 minutes until kale is tender.
6. Season with salt and pepper.
7. Serve the white bean and kale soup hot, garnished with grated Parmesan cheese if desired.
   Nutritional Info (per serving): Calories: 220 | Fat: 7g | Carbs: 30g | Protein: 10g
   Student Vegetarian Function: White bean and kale soup is a nutritious and comforting dish that's perfect for chilly days.

EDAMAME SALAD

Prep: 10 mins | Cook: 5 mins | Serves: 4

INGREDIENTS:

- 2 cups frozen edamame, thawed
- 1 bell pepper, diced
- 1 cucumber, diced
- 1/4 cup chopped red onion
- 2 tablespoons chopped fresh cilantro or parsley
- 2 tablespoons rice vinegar
- 1 tablespoon soy sauce
- 1 tablespoon sesame oil
- 1 teaspoon honey or agave syrup (optional)
- Sesame seeds, for garnish

INSTRUCTIONS:

1. Cook edamame according to package instructions if using frozen.
2. In a large bowl, combine cooked edamame, diced bell pepper, diced cucumber, chopped red onion, and chopped fresh cilantro or parsley.
3. In a small bowl, whisk together rice vinegar, soy sauce, sesame oil, and honey (if using).
4. Pour the dressing over the salad and toss to combine.
5. Garnish with sesame seeds before serving.
   Nutritional Info (per serving): Calories: 160 | Fat: 7g | Carbs: 16g | Protein: 9g
   Student Vegetarian Function: Edamame salad is a refreshing and protein-packed dish that's great for lunch or as a side.

THREE BEAN CHILI

Prep: 10 mins | Cook: 30 mins | Serves: 4

INGREDIENTS:

- 1 tablespoon olive oil
- 1 onion, diced
- 3 cloves garlic, minced
- 1 bell pepper, diced
- 1 zucchini, diced
- 1 can (15 oz) kidney beans, drained and rinsed
- 1 can (15 oz) black beans, drained and rinsed
- 1 can (15 oz) cannellini beans, drained and rinsed
- 1 can (14 oz) diced tomatoes
- 2 tablespoons tomato paste
- 2 cups vegetable broth
- 2 teaspoons chili powder
- 1 teaspoon cumin
- Salt and pepper, to taste
- Chopped fresh cilantro, for garnish

INSTRUCTIONS:

1. Heat olive oil in a large pot over medium heat.
2. Add diced onion and minced garlic. Sauté until onion is translucent.
3. Stir in diced bell pepper and diced zucchini. Cook for 5-7 minutes until vegetables start to soften.
4. Add kidney beans, black beans, cannellini beans, diced tomatoes, tomato paste, vegetable broth, chili powder, cumin, salt, and pepper to the pot.
5. Bring to a boil, then reduce heat and simmer for 20-25 minutes, stirring occasionally.
6. Adjust seasoning if needed.
7. Serve the three-bean chili hot, garnished with chopped fresh cilantro.
   Nutritional Info (per serving): Calories: 320 | Fat: 4g | Carbs: 56g | Protein: 17g
   Student Vegetarian Function: Three bean chili is a hearty and satisfying dish that's perfect for meal prep.

CHICKPEA SANDWICHES 3 WAYS

Prep: 10 mins | Cook: 0 mins | Serves: 2

INGREDIENTS:

For Classic Chickpea Salad Sandwich:

- 1 can (15 oz) chickpeas, drained and rinsed
- 2 tablespoons vegan mayonnaise (or regular mayonnaise)
- 1 tablespoon Dijon mustard
- 2 tablespoons chopped celery
- Salt and pepper, to taste
- Bread slices, lettuce, and tomato for serving

For Spicy Buffalo Chickpea Sandwich:

- 1 can (15 oz) chickpeas, drained and rinsed
- 2 tablespoons buffalo sauce
- 2 tablespoons vegan mayonnaise (or regular mayonnaise)
- Bread slices, lettuce, and pickles for serving

For Curried Chickpea Salad Sandwich:

- 1 can (15 oz) chickpeas, drained and rinsed
- 2 tablespoons vegan mayonnaise (or regular mayonnaise)
- 1 tablespoon curry powder
- 1 tablespoon chopped fresh cilantro
- Bread slices, lettuce, and cucumber for serving

INSTRUCTIONS:

1. For each variation, mash chickpeas in a bowl using a fork or potato masher.
2. Add the respective ingredients for each sandwich variation (mayonnaise, mustard, celery for classic; buffalo sauce for spicy buffalo; curry powder and cilantro for curried). Mix until well combined.
3. Spread the chickpea mixture onto bread slices.
4. Top with lettuce, tomato, pickles, or cucumber depending on the variation.
5. Serve the chickpea sandwiches immediately.
   Nutritional Info (per serving for Classic Chickpea Salad Sandwich): Calories: 320 | Fat: 10g | Carbs: 45g | Protein: 15g
   Student Vegetarian Function: Chickpea sandwiches offer versatility and are great for quick lunches or on-the-go meals.

LENTIL MEATLOAF

Prep: 15 mins | Cook: 45 mins | Serves: 4

INGREDIENTS:

- 1 cup cooked lentils (200g)
- 1 onion, finely chopped
- 2 cloves garlic, minced

- 1 carrot, grated
- 1 celery stalk, finely chopped
- 1/2 cup breadcrumbs (60g)
- 1/4 cup ketchup
- 2 tablespoons soy sauce
- 1 tablespoon Dijon mustard
- 1 tablespoon Worcestershire sauce (optional)
- Salt and pepper, to taste
- Cooking spray or olive oil, for greasing

INSTRUCTIONS:

1. Preheat the oven to 350°F (175°C). Grease a loaf pan with cooking spray or olive oil.
2. In a skillet, sauté chopped onion, minced garlic, grated carrot, and chopped celery until softened.
3. In a large bowl, combine cooked lentils, sautéed vegetables, breadcrumbs, ketchup, soy sauce, Dijon mustard, Worcestershire sauce (if using), salt, and pepper.
4. Mix until well combined, then transfer the mixture into the greased loaf pan.
5. Bake for 40-45 minutes until the lentil meatloaf is firm and golden on the outside.
6. Let it cool slightly before slicing and serving.
   Nutritional Info (per serving): Calories: 280 | Fat: 5g | Carbs: 45g | Protein: 15g
   Student Vegetarian Function: Lentil meatloaf is a nutritious and comforting twist on a classic dish.

LENTIL SLOPPY JOES

Prep: 10 mins | Cook: 20 mins | Serves: 4

INGREDIENTS:

- 1 cup cooked lentils (200g)
- 1 onion, diced
- 1 bell pepper, diced
- 2 cloves garlic, minced
- 1 can (14 oz) crushed tomatoes
- 2 tablespoons tomato paste
- 2 tablespoons maple syrup or brown sugar
- 1 tablespoon Dijon mustard
- 1 tablespoon apple cider vinegar
- 1 teaspoon chili powder
- Salt and pepper, to taste
- Hamburger buns or bread rolls, for serving

INSTRUCTIONS:

1. In a skillet, sauté diced onion, diced bell pepper, and minced garlic until softened.
2. Stir in cooked lentils, crushed tomatoes, tomato paste, maple syrup or brown sugar, Dijon mustard, apple cider vinegar, chili powder, salt, and pepper.
3. Simmer for 15-20 minutes until the mixture thickens and flavors combine.
4. Adjust seasoning if needed.

5. Serve the lentil sloppy joes on hamburger buns or bread rolls.
    Nutritional Info (per serving without bun): Calories: 240 | Fat: 1g | Carbs: 50g | Protein: 12g
    Student Vegetarian Function: Lentil sloppy joes are a fun and flavorful twist on a classic sandwich.

WHITE BEAN DIP

Prep: 10 mins | Cook: 0 mins | Serves: 4

INGREDIENTS:

- 1 can (15 oz) cannellini beans, drained and rinsed
- 2 cloves garlic, minced
- Juice of 1 lemon
- 2 tablespoons olive oil
- 1/2 teaspoon ground cumin
- Salt and pepper, to taste
- Chopped fresh parsley or paprika, for garnish
- Raw vegetables, pita bread, or tortilla chips, for serving

INSTRUCTIONS:

1. In a food processor, combine cannellini beans, minced garlic, lemon juice, olive oil, ground cumin, salt, and pepper.
2. Blend until smooth and creamy, adding a splash of water if needed to reach desired consistency.
3. Adjust seasoning to taste.
4. Transfer the white bean dip to a serving bowl.
5. Garnish with chopped fresh parsley or paprika.
6. Serve with raw vegetables, pita bread, or tortilla chips.
    Nutritional Info (per serving): Calories: 180 | Fat: 7g | Carbs: 22g | Protein: 8g
    Student Vegetarian Function: White bean dip is a quick and easy appetizer or snack that's perfect for sharing.

TOFU SCRAMBLE 3 WAYS

Prep: 10 mins | Cook: 15 mins | Serves: 2

INGREDIENTS:

- 1 block (14 oz) firm tofu, drained and pressed
  For Mexican Tofu Scramble.
- 1/2 bell pepper, diced
- 1/2 onion, diced
- 1 teaspoon chili powder
- Salt and pepper, to taste
  For Spinach & Feta Tofu Scramble:
- 1 cup fresh spinach, chopped
- 1/4 cup crumbled feta cheese
  For Mediterranean Tofu Scramble:
- 1/4 cup sliced sun-dried tomatoes
- 2 tablespoons chopped fresh basil

INSTRUCTIONS:

1. Crumble the pressed tofu into a bowl.

2. For Mexican Tofu Scramble:

   Sauté bell pepper and onion in a skillet until softened. Add crumbled tofu, chili powder, salt, and pepper. Cook until heated through.

3. For Spinach & Feta Tofu Scramble:

   Add chopped spinach to a skillet and cook until wilted. Stir in crumbled tofu and feta cheese. Cook until warmed.

4. For Mediterranean Tofu Scramble:

   Sauté sun-dried tomatoes in a skillet. Add crumbled tofu and chopped basil. Cook until combined and heated.

6. Serve each tofu scramble variation hot with toast or tortillas.
   Nutritional Info (per serving): Calories: 220 | Fat: 12g | Carbs: 8g | Protein: 20g
   Student Vegetarian Function: Tofu scrambles are quick, customizable breakfast options packed with protein.

CRISPY BAKED TOFU

Prep: 10 mins | Cook: 25 mins | Serves: 4

INGREDIENTS:

- 1 block (14 oz) extra-firm tofu, drained and pressed
- 2 tablespoons soy sauce
- 1 tablespoon maple syrup
- 1 tablespoon sesame oil
- 1 tablespoon cornstarch
- Salt and pepper, to taste

INSTRUCTIONS:

1. Preheat the oven to 400°F (200°C) and line a baking sheet with parchment paper.
2. Cut pressed tofu into cubes and place in a bowl.
3. In a separate bowl, whisk together soy sauce, maple syrup, sesame oil, cornstarch, salt, and pepper.
4. Pour the marinade over the tofu cubes and toss to coat evenly.
5. Arrange tofu cubes on the prepared baking sheet in a single layer.
6. Bake for 20-25 minutes, flipping halfway through, until tofu is golden and crispy.
7. Serve crispy baked tofu hot with rice or noodles.
   Nutritional Info (per serving): Calories: 180 | Fat: 8g | Carbs: 8g | Protein: 18g
   Student Vegetarian Function: Crispy baked tofu is a versatile protein option for salads, bowls, or wraps.

TERIYAKI TOFU STIR FRY

Prep: 15 mins | Cook: 15 mins | Serves: 4

INGREDIENTS:

- 1 block (14 oz) firm tofu, drained and pressed
- 1 cup broccoli florets
- 1 bell pepper, sliced
- 1 carrot, sliced
- 1/2 onion, sliced
- 2 cloves garlic, minced
- 1/4 cup teriyaki sauce
- 2 tablespoons soy sauce
- 1 tablespoon sesame oil
- Cooked rice or noodles, for serving

INSTRUCTIONS:

1. Cut pressed tofu into cubes.
2. Heat sesame oil in a large skillet or wok over medium-high heat.
3. Add tofu cubes and cook until golden brown on all sides. Remove tofu from the skillet and set aside.
4. In the same skillet, sauté garlic, broccoli, bell pepper, carrot, and onion until tender-crisp.
5. Return tofu to the skillet and add teriyaki sauce and soy sauce.

6. Cook for 2-3 minutes until everything is heated through and well coated.
7. Serve teriyaki tofu stir fry hot over cooked rice or noodles.
   Nutritional Info (per serving): Calories: 250 | Fat: 10g | Carbs: 22g | Protein: 18g
   Student Vegetarian Function: Teriyaki tofu stir fry is a flavorful and satisfying meal that's easy to customize with your favorite vegetables.

TOFU TACOS

Prep: 15 mins | Cook: 15 mins | Serves: 4

INGREDIENTS:

- 1 block (14 oz) extra-firm tofu, drained and pressed
- 1 tablespoon taco seasoning
- 1 tablespoon olive oil
- 8 small corn or flour tortillas
- Toppings: shredded lettuce, diced tomatoes, salsa, avocado, cilantro

INSTRUCTIONS:

1. Crumble pressed tofu into a bowl and toss with taco seasoning.
2. Heat olive oil in a skillet over medium heat.
3. Add seasoned tofu to the skillet and cook until heated through and slightly crispy.
4. Warm tortillas in a dry skillet or microwave.
5. Assemble tofu tacos with crumbled tofu and desired toppings.
6. Serve tofu tacos hot with lime wedges on the side.
   Nutritional Info (per serving, 2 tacos): Calories: 280 | Fat: 10g | Carbs: 30g | Protein: 15g
   Student Vegetarian Function: Tofu tacos are a fun and protein-packed twist on traditional tacos.

TOFU CURRY

Prep: 15 mins | Cook: 25 mins | Serves: 4

INGREDIENTS:

- 1 block (14 oz) firm tofu, drained and pressed
- 1 tablespoon curry powder
- 1 can (14 oz) coconut milk
- 1 bell pepper, sliced
- 1 zucchini, sliced
- 1 onion, sliced
- 2 tablespoons soy sauce
- Cooked rice, for serving

INSTRUCTIONS:

1. Cut pressed tofu into cubes and toss with curry powder.
2. Heat a large skillet or pot over medium heat.
3. Add tofu cubes and cook until golden brown on all sides. Remove tofu from the skillet and set aside.

4. In the same skillet, sauté bell pepper, zucchini, and onion until tender.
5. Return tofu to the skillet and add coconut milk and soy sauce.
6. Simmer for 10-15 minutes until vegetables are cooked and tofu is infused with curry flavor.
7. Serve tofu curry hot over cooked rice.
   Nutritional Info (per serving): Calories: 320 | Fat: 22g | Carbs: 16g | Protein: 16g
   Student Vegetarian Function: Tofu curry is a comforting and aromatic dish that's perfect for dinner.

TOFU EGG SALAD

Prep: 10 mins | Cook: 0 mins | Serves: 2

INGREDIENTS:

- 1 block (14 oz) firm tofu, drained and pressed
- 2 tablespoons vegan mayonnaise (or regular mayonnaise)
- 1 tablespoon Dijon mustard
- 1 tablespoon chopped fresh dill (or dried dill)
- Salt and pepper, to taste
- Sandwich bread or lettuce wraps, for serving

INSTRUCTIONS:

1. Crumble pressed tofu into a bowl.
2. Add vegan mayonnaise, Dijon mustard, chopped dill, salt, and pepper to the bowl. Mix until well combined.
3. Serve tofu egg salad as a sandwich filling or wrap filling.
   Nutritional Info (per serving): Calories: 220 | Fat: 15g | Carbs: 4g | Protein: 15g
   Student Vegetarian Function: Tofu egg salad is a protein-rich alternative to traditional egg salad.

GENERAL TSO'S TOFU

Prep: 15 mins | Cook: 20 mins | Serves: 4

INGREDIENTS:

- 1 block (14 oz) extra-firm tofu, drained and pressed
- 1/4 cup cornstarch
- 2 tablespoons soy sauce
- 2 tablespoons hoisin sauce
- 2 tablespoons rice vinegar
- 1 tablespoon maple syrup
- 1 tablespoon sesame oil
- 2 cloves garlic, minced
- 1-inch piece ginger, minced
- Red pepper flakes, to taste
- Cooked rice, for serving
- Steamed broccoli florets, for serving

INSTRUCTIONS:

1. Cut pressed tofu into cubes and toss with cornstarch until coated.
2. Heat sesame oil in a large skillet over medium-high heat.
3. Add tofu cubes to the skillet and cook until crispy and golden brown. Remove tofu from the skillet and set aside.
4. In the same skillet, sauté minced garlic, minced ginger, and red pepper flakes until fragrant.
5. Whisk together soy sauce, hoisin sauce, rice vinegar, and maple syrup in a bowl.
6. Pour the sauce into the skillet and bring to a simmer.
7. Return crispy tofu to the skillet and toss to coat with the sauce.
8. Serve General Tso's tofu hot over cooked rice with steamed broccoli.
   Nutritional Info (per serving): Calories: 320 | Fat: 12g | Carbs: 38g | Protein: 18g
   Student Vegetarian Function: General Tso's tofu is a flavorful and satisfying dish inspired by Chinese takeout.

TEMPEH REUBENS

Prep: 10 mins | Cook: 10 mins | Serves: 2

INGREDIENTS:

- 1 package (8 oz) tempeh, sliced
- 1/4 cup sauerkraut
- 2 tablespoons Russian or Thousand Island dressing
- 4 slices rye or pumpernickel bread
- Butter or vegan spread, for grilling

INSTRUCTIONS:

1. Heat butter or vegan spread in a skillet over medium heat.
2. Add tempeh slices to the skillet and cook until browned and crispy on both sides.
3. Toast bread slices in the skillet until golden brown.
4. Spread Russian or Thousand Island dressing on one side of each bread slice.
5. Layer tempeh slices, sauerkraut, and additional dressing on the bread slices to assemble the sandwiches.
6. Grill sandwiches in the skillet until heated through and crispy on the outside.
7. Serve tempeh Reubens hot with pickles or coleslaw.
   Nutritional Info (per serving): Calories: 380 | Fat: 14g | Carbs: 45g | Protein: 20g
   Student Vegetarian Function: Tempeh Reubens are a tasty vegetarian twist on the classic deli sandwich.

TEMPEH BACON

Prep: 10 mins | Cook: 10 mins | Serves: 4

INGREDIENTS:

- 1 package (8 oz) tempeh, thinly sliced
- 2 tablespoons soy sauce
- 1 tablespoon maple syrup
- 1/2 teaspoon liquid smoke (optional)

- 1 tablespoon olive oil

INSTRUCTIONS:

1. In a shallow dish, whisk together soy sauce, maple syrup, and liquid smoke (if using).
2. Add tempeh slices to the marinade and let sit for 5 minutes.
3. Heat olive oil in a skillet over medium heat.
4. Add marinated tempeh slices to the skillet and cook until crispy and browned on both sides, about 3-4 minutes per side.
5. Serve tempeh bacon hot as a breakfast side or in sandwiches.
   Nutritional Info (per serving): Calories: 220 | Fat: 12g | Carbs: 12g | Protein: 16g
   Student Vegetarian Function: Tempeh bacon is a smoky and savory alternative to traditional bacon.

TEMPEH BURGER

Prep: 15 mins | Cook: 15 mins | Serves: 4

INGREDIENTS:

- 1 package (8 oz) tempeh, crumbled
- 1/2 cup breadcrumbs
- 1/4 cup chopped onion
- 2 cloves garlic, minced
- 2 tablespoons soy sauce
- 1 tablespoon Dijon mustard
- 1 tablespoon BBQ sauce
- Salt and pepper, to taste
- Burger buns, lettuce, tomato, and condiments for serving

INSTRUCTIONS:

1. In a bowl, combine crumbled tempeh, breadcrumbs, chopped onion, minced garlic, soy sauce, Dijon mustard, BBQ sauce, salt, and pepper.
2. Mix until well combined, then shape into burger patties.
3. Heat olive oil in a skillet over medium heat.
4. Cook tempeh burgers for 3-4 minutes on each side until browned and heated through.
5. Serve tempeh burgers on buns with lettuce, tomato, and your favorite condiments.
   Nutritional Info (per serving): Calories: 280 | Fat: 10g | Carbs: 32g | Protein: 18g
   Student Vegetarian Function: Tempeh burgers are a hearty and satisfying option for lunch or dinner.

BBQ TEMPEH

Prep: 10 mins | Cook: 20 mins | Serves: 4

INGREDIENTS:

- 1 package (8 oz) tempeh, sliced
- 1/2 cup BBQ sauce
- 1 tablespoon olive oil

- Salt and pepper, to taste

INSTRUCTIONS:

1. Preheat the oven to 375°F (190°C) and line a baking sheet with parchment paper.
2. Toss tempeh slices with olive oil, salt, and pepper.
3. Arrange tempeh slices on the prepared baking sheet.
4. Brush tempeh slices with BBQ sauce, ensuring they are evenly coated.
5. Bake for 15-20 minutes, flipping halfway through, until tempeh is caramelized and heated through.
6. Serve BBQ tempeh hot with coleslaw or cornbread.
   Nutritional Info (per serving): Calories: 240 | Fat: 9g | Carbs: 22g | Protein: 18g
   Student Vegetarian Function: BBQ tempeh is a sweet and savory dish that's perfect for summer cookouts.

TEMPEH WINGS

Prep: 15 mins | Cook: 30 mins | Serves: 4

INGREDIENTS:

- 1 package (8 oz) tempeh, cut into strips or triangles
- 1/2 cup buffalo sauce (or BBQ sauce for BBQ wings)
- 2 tablespoons olive oil
- Ranch or blue cheese dressing, for dipping

INSTRUCTIONS:

1. Preheat the oven to 375°F (190°C) and line a baking sheet with parchment paper.
2. Toss tempeh strips or triangles with olive oil.
3. Arrange tempeh on the prepared baking sheet and bake for 15 minutes.
4. Remove tempeh from the oven and brush with buffalo sauce or BBQ sauce.
5. Return tempeh to the oven and bake for an additional 15 minutes until crispy.
6. Serve tempeh wings hot with ranch or blue cheese dressing for dipping.
   Nutritional Info (per serving): Calories: 260 | Fat: 14g | Carbs: 15g | Protein: 18g
   Student Vegetarian Function: Tempeh wings are a fun and flavorful appetizer or snack for game day.

TEMPEH MEATBALLS

Prep: 15 mins | Cook: 25 mins | Serves: 4

INGREDIENTS:

- 1 package (8 oz) tempeh, crumbled
- 1/2 cup breadcrumbs
- 1/4 cup grated Parmesan cheese (or nutritional yeast for vegan)
- 1 egg (or flaxseed egg for vegan)
- 2 cloves garlic, minced
- 1 tablespoon Italian seasoning
- Salt and pepper, to taste
- Marinara sauce, for serving

- Cooked spaghetti, for serving

INSTRUCTIONS:

1. Preheat the oven to 375°F (190°C) and line a baking sheet with parchment paper.
2. In a bowl, combine crumbled tempeh, breadcrumbs, grated Parmesan cheese, egg, minced garlic, Italian seasoning, salt, and pepper.
3. Mix until well combined, then shape into meatballs.
4. Arrange tempeh meatballs on the prepared baking sheet.
5. Bake for 20-25 minutes until meatballs are golden and cooked through.
6. Serve tempeh meatballs hot with marinara sauce and cooked spaghetti.
   Nutritional Info (per serving): Calories: 280 | Fat: 12g | Carbs: 20g | Protein: 20g
   Student Vegetarian Function: Tempeh meatballs are a tasty and protein-packed alternative to traditional meatballs.

COCONUT CRUSTED TEMPEH

Prep: 15 mins | Cook: 20 mins | Serves: 4

INGREDIENTS:

- 1 package (8 oz) tempeh, sliced
- 1/2 cup coconut milk
- 1 cup breadcrumbs
- 1/2 cup shredded coconut
- Salt and pepper, to taste
- Cooking spray or olive oil

INSTRUCTIONS:

1. Preheat the oven to 375°F (190°C) and line a baking sheet with parchment paper.
2. In a bowl, marinate tempeh slices in coconut milk for 10 minutes.
3. In a separate bowl, combine breadcrumbs, shredded coconut, salt, and pepper.
4. Dip each tempeh slice in the breadcrumb mixture, ensuring they are evenly coated.
5. Arrange tempeh slices on the prepared baking sheet and lightly spray with cooking spray or drizzle with olive oil.
6. Bake for 15-20 minutes until coconut crust is golden and crispy.
7. Serve coconut crusted tempeh hot with mango salsa or sweet chili sauce.
   Nutritional Info (per serving): Calories: 320 | Fat: 16g | Carbs: 28g | Protein: 18g
   Student Vegetarian Function: Coconut crusted tempeh is a tropical and satisfying dish that's perfect for dinner.

VEGGIE FRITTERS 3 WAYS

Prep: 15 mins | Cook: 15 mins | Serves: 4

INGREDIENTS:

- 2 cups grated zucchini or carrots (US) / courgetti or carrots (UK)
- 1 cup chickpea flour (US & UK)
- 1/4 cup chopped fresh herbs (parsley, cilantro, or dill)
- Salt and pepper, to taste
- Cooking oil, for frying

INSTRUCTIONS:

1. In a bowl, combine grated veggies, chickpea flour, chopped herbs, salt, and pepper.
2. Mix until well combined to form a thick batter.
3. Heat oil in a skillet over medium heat.
4. Drop spoonsful of the batter into the skillet and flatten slightly with a spatula.
5. Cook for 3-4 minutes on each side until golden and crispy.
6. Serve veggie fritters hot with yogurt or dipping sauce.
   Nutritional Info (per serving): Calories: 180 | Fat: 8g | Carbs: 22g | Protein: 6g
   Student Vegetarian Function: Veggie fritters are a quick and versatile dinner option that can be customized with different vegetables.

BAKED PASTA 3 WAYS

Prep: 15 mins | Cook: 30 mins | Serves: 4

INGREDIENTS:

- 8 oz (225g) pasta (penne, fusilli, or spaghetti)
- 1 jar (24 oz) marinara sauce (US & UK)
- 1 cup shredded mozzarella cheese (US & UK)
  For Spinach & Ricotta Pasta Bake:
- 1 cup chopped spinach
- 1 cup ricotta cheese
  For Mushroom & Spinach Pasta Bake:
- 1 cup sliced mushrooms
- 1 cup chopped spinach
  For Roasted Vegetable Pasta Bake:
- 1 cup chopped roasted vegetables (bell peppers, zucchini, eggplant)

INSTRUCTIONS:

1. Preheat the oven to 375°F (190°C) and grease a baking dish.

2. Cook pasta according to package instructions, then drain.
3. In a large bowl, combine cooked pasta with marinara sauce and desired mix-ins (spinach, ricotta, mushrooms, roasted vegetables).
4. Transfer pasta mixture to the baking dish and top with shredded mozzarella cheese.
5. Bake for 20-25 minutes until cheese is bubbly and golden.
6. Serve baked pasta hot with garlic bread or salad.
   Nutritional Info (per serving): Calories: 380 | Fat: 12g | Carbs: 52g | Protein: 18g
   Student Vegetarian Function: Baked pasta is a comforting and crowd-pleasing dinner option that's easy to customize.

VEGGIE PIZZA 4 WAYS

Prep: 15 mins | Cook: 15 mins | Serves: 4

INGREDIENTS:

- 4 small pre-made pizza crusts (US & UK)
- 1 cup tomato sauce (US & UK)
- 2 cups shredded mozzarella cheese (US & UK)
  Toppings:
- Margherita Pizza: Fresh basil leaves, sliced tomatoes
- Veggie Supreme Pizza: Bell peppers, onions, olives, mushrooms
- Pesto Veggie Pizza: Pesto sauce, cherry tomatoes, spinach
- BBQ Veggie Pizza: BBQ sauce, sliced red onions, corn kernels

INSTRUCTIONS:

1. Preheat the oven to 425°F (220°C).
2. Place pizza crusts on a baking sheet.
3. Spread tomato sauce evenly over each crust.
4. Top with shredded mozzarella cheese and desired toppings for each pizza variation.
5. Bake for 12-15 minutes until crust is golden and cheese is melted.
6. Slice and serve veggie pizzas hot.
   Nutritional Info (per serving, Margherita Pizza): Calories: 280 | Fat: 10g | Carbs: 32g | Protein: 14g
   Student Vegetarian Function: Veggie pizza is a quick and customizable dinner option perfect for busy evenings.

VEGGIE FAJITAS

Prep: 15 mins | Cook: 15 mins | Serves: 4

INGREDIENTS:

- 2 bell peppers, sliced (US & UK)
- 1 onion, sliced (US & UK)
- 1 zucchini, sliced (US) / courgetti, sliced (UK)
- 1 cup canned black beans, drained and rinsed (US & UK)
- 1 tablespoon taco seasoning (US & UK)
- 8 small flour tortillas (US & UK)

- Toppings: salsa, guacamole, sour cream

INSTRUCTIONS:

1. Heat oil in a skillet over medium-high heat.
2. Add sliced bell peppers, onion, and zucchini to the skillet.
3. Sauté for 5-7 minutes until vegetables are tender-crisp.
4. Stir in black beans and taco seasoning, cook for an additional 2-3 minutes.
5. Warm tortillas in a dry skillet or microwave.
6. Serve veggie fajita mixture in tortillas with desired toppings.
   Nutritional Info (per serving, without toppings): Calories: 280 | Fat: 5g | Carbs: 48g | Protein: 10g
   Student Vegetarian Function: Veggie fajitas are a colorful and flavorful Tex-Mex dinner option that's ready in minutes.

STUFFED POTATOES 4 WAYS

Prep: 10 mins | Cook: 45 mins | Serves: 4

INGREDIENTS:

- 4 large baking potatoes (US & UK)
  For Broccoli & Cheese Stuffed Potatoes:
- 1 cup steamed broccoli florets
- 1 cup shredded cheddar cheese
  For Mexican Stuffed Potatoes:
- 1 cup cooked black beans
- 1 cup salsa
- 1/2 cup shredded Monterey Jack cheese
  For Mediterranean Stuffed Potatoes:
- 1 cup chopped tomatoes
- 1/2 cup crumbled feta cheese
- 2 tablespoons chopped fresh basil
  For Spinach & Artichoke Stuffed Potatoes:
- 1 cup cooked spinach
- 1/2 cup chopped artichoke hearts
- 1/2 cup cream cheese

INSTRUCTIONS:

1. Preheat the oven to 400°F (200°C).
2. Scrub potatoes clean and prick with a fork.
3. Bake potatoes directly on the oven rack for 45-60 minutes until tender.
4. Slice potatoes open and fluff the insides with a fork.
5. Stuff each potato with desired fillings (broccoli & cheese, Mexican, Mediterranean, spinach & artichoke).
6. Return stuffed potatoes to the oven for 5-10 minutes until cheese is melted and fillings are heated through.
7. Serve stuffed potatoes hot.

Nutritional Info (per serving, Broccoli & Cheese Stuffed Potato): Calories: 320 | Fat: 10g | Carbs: 48g | Protein: 12g

Student Vegetarian Function: Stuffed potatoes are a hearty and satisfying dinner option that can be customized with favorite toppings.

STUFFED PEPPERS 3 WAYS

Prep: 15 mins | Cook: 30 mins | Serves: 4

INGREDIENTS:

- 4 large bell peppers (any color) (US & UK)
  For Quinoa & Black Bean Stuffed Peppers:
- 1 cup cooked quinoa
- 1 cup canned black beans, drained and rinsed
- 1 cup diced tomatoes
- 1 teaspoon chili powder
- 1/2 cup shredded cheddar cheese
  For Lentil & Rice Stuffed Peppers:
- 1 cup cooked brown rice
- 1 cup cooked lentils
- 1 cup tomato sauce
- 1 teaspoon Italian seasoning
- 1/2 cup grated Parmesan cheese (or nutritional yeast for vegan)
  For Spinach & Feta Stuffed Peppers:
- 1 cup chopped spinach
- 1/2 cup crumbled feta cheese
- 1/4 cup chopped sun-dried tomatoes
- 1/4 cup pine nuts (optional)

INSTRUCTIONS:

1. Preheat the oven to 375°F (190°C) and grease a baking dish.
2. Cut the tops off the bell peppers and remove seeds and membranes.
3. In a bowl, mix together the ingredients for each stuffing variation.
4. Stuff the bell peppers with the prepared fillings and place them in the baking dish.
5. Cover the dish with foil and bake for 20-25 minutes.
6. Remove the foil and bake for an additional 5-10 minutes until peppers are tender.
7. Serve stuffed peppers hot with a side salad.
   Nutritional Info (per serving, Quinoa & Black Bean Stuffed Pepper): Calories: 320 | Fat: 9g | Carbs: 48g | Protein: 14g
   Student Vegetarian Function: Stuffed peppers are a wholesome and versatile dinner option that can be filled with various grains, beans, and vegetables.

VEGGIE POT PIE

Prep: 15 mins | Cook: 30 mins | Serves: 4

INGREDIENTS:

- 1 sheet pre-made puff pastry (US & UK)
- 2 cups mixed frozen vegetables (peas, carrots, corn) (US & UK)
- 1 cup diced potatoes (US & UK)
- 1 onion, chopped (US & UK)
- 1 garlic clove, minced (US & UK)
- 1 cup vegetable broth (US & UK)
- 1/2 cup milk (US & UK)
- 2 tablespoons all-purpose flour (US & UK)
- 2 tablespoons butter (US & UK)
- Salt and pepper, to taste

INSTRUCTIONS:

1. Preheat the oven to 400°F (200°C).
2. In a skillet, melt butter over medium heat.
3. Add chopped onion and garlic, sauté until translucent.
4. Stir in diced potatoes and mixed vegetables.
5. Sprinkle flour over the vegetables, mix well to coat.
6. Gradually pour in vegetable broth and milk, stirring constantly until thickened.
7. Season with salt and pepper to taste.
8. Transfer the vegetable mixture to a baking dish.
9. Place the puff pastry over the filling, trimming excess dough.
10. Bake for 20-25 minutes until pastry is golden and filling is bubbly.
11. Serve veggie pot pie hot.
    Nutritional Info (per serving): Calories: 380 | Fat: 18g | Carbs: 48g | Protein: 8g
    Student Vegetarian Function: Veggie pot pie is a comforting and hearty dinner option that's perfect for chilly evenings.

VEGGIE ENCHILADAS

Prep: 20 mins | Cook: 25 mins | Serves: 4

INGREDIENTS:

- 8 small flour tortillas (US & UK)
- 2 cups mixed vegetables (bell peppers, onions, zucchini) (US & UK)
- 1 cup cooked black beans (US & UK)
- 1 cup enchilada sauce (US & UK)
- 1 cup shredded cheese (cheddar or Monterey Jack) (US & UK)
- 1 tablespoon olive oil
- Salt and pepper, to taste
- Toppings: chopped cilantro, sour cream, salsa

INSTRUCTIONS:

1. Preheat the oven to 375°F (190°C).
2. In a skillet, heat olive oil over medium-high heat.
3. Add mixed vegetables and sauté until tender-crisp.
4. Stir in black beans, salt, and pepper.
5. Spread a spoonful of enchilada sauce on each tortilla.
6. Spoon vegetable and bean mixture onto each tortilla, roll up tightly.
7. Place rolled enchiladas seam side down in a baking dish.
8. Pour remaining enchilada sauce over the enchiladas and sprinkle with shredded cheese.
9. Bake for 20-25 minutes until cheese is melted and bubbly.
10. Serve veggie enchiladas hot with desired toppings.
    Nutritional Info (per serving): Calories: 380 | Fat: 15g | Carbs: 48g | Protein: 14g
    Student Vegetarian Function: Veggie enchiladas are a flavorful and satisfying dinner option that's easy to prepare.

EGGPLANT PARMESAN 3 WAYS

Prep: 20 mins | Cook: 30 mins | Serves: 4

INGREDIENTS:

- 1 large eggplant (US & UK)
- 1 cup breadcrumbs (US & UK)
- 1/2 cup grated Parmesan cheese (US & UK)
- 2 eggs, beaten (US & UK)
- 2 cups marinara sauce (US & UK)
- 1 cup shredded mozzarella cheese (US & UK)
  For Classic Eggplant Parmesan:
- 1 teaspoon dried Italian seasoning
  For Pesto Eggplant Parmesan:
- 1/4 cup prepared pesto sauce
  For Spinach & Ricotta Eggplant Parmesan:
- 1 cup chopped spinach
- 1 cup ricotta cheese

INSTRUCTIONS:

1. Preheat the oven to 400°F (200°C) and grease a baking sheet.
2. Slice eggplant into 1/4-inch-thick rounds.
3. Dip eggplant slices in beaten eggs, then coat in breadcrumbs mixed with grated Parmesan cheese.
4. Arrange breaded eggplant slices on the baking sheet and bake for 20 minutes until golden and crispy.
5. In a baking dish, spread a thin layer of marinara sauce.
6. Arrange baked eggplant slices in the dish, layering with marinara sauce and desired toppings (Italian seasoning, pesto, spinach & ricotta).
7. Sprinkle shredded mozzarella cheese over the top.
8. Bake for 20-25 minutes until cheese is melted and bubbly.

9. Serve eggplant Parmesan hot with garlic bread or salad.
    Nutritional Info (per serving, Classic Eggplant Parmesan): Calories: 320 | Fat: 15g | Carbs: 32g | Protein: 16g
    Student Vegetarian Function: Eggplant Parmesan is a classic Italian-inspired dish that's perfect for a
    comforting dinner.

ROASTED VEGGIE PLATTER

Prep: 15 mins | Cook: 25 mins | Serves: 4

INGREDIENTS:

- 2 bell peppers, sliced (US & UK)
- 1 large zucchini, sliced (US) / courgetti, sliced (UK)
- 1 large eggplant, diced (US & UK)
- 1-pint cherry tomatoes (US & UK)
- 1 red onion, sliced (US & UK)
- 2 tablespoons olive oil
- 1 tablespoon balsamic vinegar
- 2 cloves garlic, minced (US & UK)
- Salt and pepper, to taste
- Fresh herbs (parsley, basil) for garnish

INSTRUCTIONS:

1. Preheat the oven to 425°F (220°C) and grease a baking sheet.
2. Arrange sliced vegetables and cherry tomatoes on the baking sheet.
3. In a small bowl, whisk together olive oil, balsamic vinegar, minced garlic, salt, and pepper.
4. Drizzle the dressing over the vegetables and toss to coat evenly.
5. Roast in the oven for 20-25 minutes until vegetables are tender and caramelized.
6. Transfer roasted veggies to a serving platter and garnish with fresh herbs.
7. Serve roasted veggie platter as a main course or side dish.
    Nutritional Info (per serving): Calories: 180 | Fat: 7g | Carbs: 28g | Protein: 5g
    Student Vegetarian Function: Roasted veggie platter is a simple yet delicious dinner option that highlights
    the natural flavors of seasonal vegetables.

CAULIFLOWER BUFFALO WINGS

Prep: 15 mins | Cook: 25 mins | Serves: 4

INGREDIENTS:

- 1 head cauliflower, cut into florets (US & UK)
- 1 cup all-purpose flour (US & UK)
- 1 cup milk (US & UK)
- 1 teaspoon garlic powder (US & UK)
- Salt and pepper, to taste
- 1 cup buffalo sauce (US & UK)
- 2 tablespoons butter (or vegan butter) (US & UK)
- Ranch or blue cheese dressing, for dipping

INSTRUCTIONS:

1. Preheat the oven to 450°F (230°C) and grease a baking sheet.
2. In a bowl, whisk together flour, milk, garlic powder, salt, and pepper to create a batter.
3. Dip cauliflower florets into the batter, coating evenly, then place on the baking sheet.
4. Bake for 20-25 minutes until cauliflower is golden and crispy.
5. In a small saucepan, melt butter and stir in buffalo sauce.
6. Toss baked cauliflower in the buffalo sauce mixture until coated.
7. Serve cauliflower buffalo wings hot with ranch or blue cheese dressing for dipping.
   Nutritional Info (per serving): Calories: 250 | Fat: 7g | Carbs: 42g | Protein: 8g
   Student Vegetarian Function: Cauliflower buffalo wings are a tasty and healthier alternative to traditional chicken wings, perfect for game nights or casual dinners.

PORTOBELLO STEAKS

Prep: 15 mins | Cook: 15 mins | Serves: 4

INGREDIENTS:

- 4 large portobello mushroom caps (US & UK)
- 1/4 cup balsamic vinegar (US & UK)
- 2 tablespoons olive oil (US & UK)
- 2 cloves garlic, minced (US & UK)
- 1 teaspoon dried thyme (US & UK)
- Salt and pepper, to taste

INSTRUCTIONS:

1. In a shallow dish, whisk together balsamic vinegar, olive oil, minced garlic, dried thyme, salt, and pepper.
2. Place portobello mushroom caps in the marinade, turning to coat both sides.
3. Let mushrooms marinate for at least 10 minutes.
4. Preheat a grill or grill pan over medium-high heat.
5. Grill portobello mushroom caps for 4-5 minutes on each side until tender.
6. Serve portobello steaks hot with your favorite side dishes.
   Nutritional Info (per serving): Calories: 90 | Fat: 7g | Carbs: 5g | Protein: 3g
   Student Vegetarian Function: Portobello steaks are a satisfying and meaty vegetarian main course, perfect for grilling or indoor cooking.

MUSHROOM WELLINGTON

Prep: 20 mins | Cook: 30 mins | Serves: 4

INGREDIENTS:

- 1 sheet pre-made puff pastry (US & UK)
- 4 large portobello mushroom caps (US & UK)
- 2 cups chopped mushrooms (button or cremini) (US & UK)
- 1 onion, finely chopped (US & UK)
- 2 cloves garlic, minced (US & UK)

- 1/2 cup breadcrumbs (US & UK)
- 2 tablespoons chopped fresh parsley (US & UK)
- Salt and pepper, to taste
- 2 tablespoons olive oil (US & UK)
- 1 egg, beaten (for egg wash)

INSTRUCTIONS:

1. Preheat the oven to 400°F (200°C) and grease a baking sheet.
2. In a skillet, heat olive oil over medium heat.
3. Add chopped onions and garlic, sauté until translucent.
4. Add chopped mushrooms and cook until softened.
5. Stir in breadcrumbs and chopped parsley, season with salt and pepper.
6. Roll out puff pastry on a floured surface and place mushroom caps in the center.
7. Spoon mushroom filling over the mushroom caps.
8. Fold the pastry over the mushrooms to form a log, sealing the edges.
9. Place the mushroom Wellington seam side down on the baking sheet.
10. Brush the pastry with beaten egg for a golden finish.
11. Bake for 25-30 minutes until pastry is golden and crispy.
12. Serve mushroom Wellington sliced with gravy or sauce.
    Nutritional Info (per serving): Calories: 350 | Fat: 20g | Carbs: 32g | Protein: 9g
    Student Vegetarian Function: Mushroom Wellington is an elegant and impressive vegetarian dish that's perfect for special occasions.

VEGGIE HAND PIES

Prep: 20 mins | Cook: 25 mins | Serves: 4

INGREDIENTS:

- 1 sheet pre-made puff pastry (US & UK)
- 2 cups mixed vegetables (peas, carrots, corn) (US & UK)
- 1 onion, finely chopped (US & UK)
- 2 cloves garlic, minced (US & UK)
- 1 tablespoon olive oil (US & UK)
- Salt and pepper, to taste
- 1/2 cup grated cheese (cheddar or mozzarella) (US & UK)
- 1 egg, beaten (for egg wash)

INSTRUCTIONS:

1. Preheat the oven to 400°F (200°C) and grease a baking sheet.
2. In a skillet, heat olive oil over medium heat.
3. Add chopped onion and garlic, sauté until translucent.
4. Add mixed vegetables and cook until tender.
5. Season with salt and pepper, then remove from heat.
6. Roll out puff pastry on a floured surface and cut into squares.
7. Spoon vegetable mixture onto one half of each pastry square.

8. Sprinkle grated cheese over the vegetables.
9. Fold the pastry over the filling, sealing the edges with a fork.
10. Place hand pies on the baking sheet and brush with beaten egg.
11. Bake for 20-25 minutes until golden and puffed.
12. Serve veggie hand pies hot or warm.

Nutritional Info (per serving): Calories: 280 | Fat: 18g | Carbs: 24g | Protein: 6g

Student Vegetarian Function: Veggie hand pies are a portable and savory dinner option that's great for on-the-go meals or picnics.

SIDES AND ROASTS

MASHED POTATOES 3 WAYS

Prep: 10 mins | Cook: 20 mins | Serves: 4

INGREDIENTS:

- 4 large potatoes, peeled and cubed (US & UK)
- Salt, to taste
  For Classic Mashed Potatoes:
- 1/4 cup butter (US & UK)
- 1/2 cup milk (US & UK)
  For Garlic Herb Mashed Potatoes:
- 2 cloves garlic, minced (US & UK)
- 2 tablespoons chopped fresh herbs (parsley, thyme, rosemary) (US & UK)
  For Cheesy Mashed Potatoes:
- 1/2 cup shredded cheddar cheese (US & UK)
- 2 tablespoons cream cheese (US & UK)

INSTRUCTIONS:

1. Place the cubed potatoes in a pot, cover with water, and add a pinch of salt.
2. Bring to a boil and cook until potatoes are fork-tender, about 15-20 minutes.
3. Drain the potatoes and return them to the pot.
4. For Classic Mashed Potatoes: Add butter and milk to the potatoes, mash until smooth.
5. For Garlic Herb Mashed Potatoes: Sauté minced garlic in butter, then add to the potatoes along with chopped herbs, mash together.
6. For Cheesy Mashed Potatoes: Stir in shredded cheddar cheese and cream cheese into the hot potatoes until melted and combined.
7. Season mashed potatoes with additional salt and pepper if needed.
8. Serve hot as a side dish with your favorite main course.
   Nutritional Info (per serving, Classic Mashed Potatoes): Calories: 250 | Fat: 10g | Carbs: 37g | Protein: 4g
   Student Vegetarian Function: Mashed potatoes are a versatile side dish that can be customized with various flavors to complement different meals.

ROASTED VEGETABLES

Prep: 10 mins | Cook: 20 mins | Serves: 4

INGREDIENTS:

- 4 cups mixed vegetables (bell peppers, zucchini, carrots, onions) (US & UK)
- 2 tablespoons olive oil (US & UK)
- Salt and pepper, to taste
- Optional: minced garlic, dried herbs (thyme, rosemary), Parmesan cheese

INSTRUCTIONS:

1. Preheat the oven to 425°F (220°C) and line a baking sheet with parchment paper.
2. Cut vegetables into bite-sized pieces and place them on the baking sheet.
3. Drizzle olive oil over the vegetables, season with salt, pepper, and any additional seasonings.
4. Toss vegetables to coat evenly with oil and seasonings.
5. Spread vegetables in a single layer on the baking sheet.
6. Roast in the oven for 15-20 minutes, stirring halfway through, until vegetables are tender and caramelized.
7. Remove from the oven and serve hot as a side dish.
   Nutritional Info (per serving): Calories: 120 | Fat: 7g | Carbs: 14g | Protein: 2g
   Student Vegetarian Function: Roasted vegetables are a simple and healthy side dish that pairs well with any main course.

ROASTED CHICKPEAS

Prep: 5 mins | Cook: 25 mins | Serves: 4

INGREDIENTS:

- 2 cans (15 oz each) chickpeas, drained and rinsed (US & UK)
- 2 tablespoons olive oil (US & UK)
- 1 teaspoon smoked paprika (US & UK)
- 1 teaspoon cumin (US & UK)
- Salt and pepper, to taste

INSTRUCTIONS:

1. Preheat the oven to 400°F (200°C) and line a baking sheet with parchment paper.
2. Pat dries the chickpeas with a kitchen towel to remove excess moisture.
3. In a bowl, toss chickpeas with olive oil, smoked paprika, cumin, salt, and pepper.
4. Spread chickpeas in a single layer on the baking sheet.
5. Roast in the oven for 20-25 minutes, shaking the pan halfway through, until chickpeas are crispy.
6. Remove from the oven and let cool slightly before serving.
7. Serve roasted chickpeas as a crunchy snack or a topping for salads and bowls.
   Nutritional Info (per serving): Calories: 180 | Fat: 7g | Carbs: 22g | Protein: 8g
   Student Vegetarian Function: Roasted chickpeas are a nutritious and satisfying snack or addition to salads, providing a crunchy texture and protein boost.

ROASTED BRUSSELS SPROUTS

Prep: 10 mins | Cook: 20 mins | Serves: 4

INGREDIENTS:

- 1 pound Brussels sprouts, trimmed and halved (US & UK)
- 2 tablespoons olive oil (US & UK)
- Salt and pepper, to taste
- Optional: balsamic vinegar, grated Parmesan cheese, chopped nuts (like pecans or almonds)

INSTRUCTIONS:

1. Preheat the oven to 400°F (200°C) and line a baking sheet with parchment paper.
2. Toss Brussels sprouts with olive oil, salt, and pepper in a bowl until coated.
3. Spread Brussels sprouts in a single layer on the baking sheet.
4. Roast in the oven for 15-20 minutes, shaking the pan halfway through, until Brussels sprouts are tender and caramelized.
5. Remove from the oven and drizzle with balsamic vinegar or sprinkle with grated Parmesan cheese and chopped nuts, if desired.
6. Serve hot as a side dish.
   Nutritional Info (per serving): Calories: 100 | Fat: 7g | Carbs: 9g | Protein: 3g
   Student Vegetarian Function: Roasted Brussels sprouts are a flavorful and nutritious side dish that complements any meal, providing a boost of vitamins and fiber.

HASSELBACK POTATOES

Prep: 15 mins | Cook: 45 mins | Serves: 4

INGREDIENTS:

- 4 large potatoes, scrubbed and thinly sliced (but not all the way through) (US & UK)
- 3 tablespoons melted butter (US & UK)
- 2 cloves garlic, minced (US & UK)
- Salt and pepper, to taste
- Optional: grated cheese, chopped herbs (parsley, chives)

INSTRUCTIONS:

1. Preheat the oven to 400°F (200°C) and grease a baking dish.
2. In a bowl, mix melted butter, minced garlic, salt, and pepper.
3. Place the sliced potatoes in the baking dish.
4. Brush the potatoes with the garlic butter mixture, making sure to get in between the slices.
5. Bake for 40-45 minutes until potatoes are crispy and tender.
6. Optional: Sprinkle grated cheese and chopped herbs over the potatoes during the last 5 minutes of baking.
7. Serve hot as a unique and delicious side dish.
   Nutritional Info (per serving): Calories: 220 | Fat: 10g | Carbs: 30g | Protein: 4g
   Student Vegetarian Function: Hasselback potatoes are a visually impressive and tasty side dish that's easy to prepare, perfect for special occasions or everyday meals.

CREAMED SPINACH

Prep: 5 mins | Cook: 10 mins | Serves: 4

INGREDIENTS:

- 1-pound fresh spinach, washed and trimmed (US & UK)
- 2 tablespoons butter (US & UK)
- 2 cloves garlic, minced (US & UK)

- 1 cup heavy cream (US) / double cream (UK)
- Salt and pepper, to taste
- Grated nutmeg, for garnish (optional)

INSTRUCTIONS:

1. In a large skillet, melt butter over medium heat.
2. Add minced garlic and sauté until fragrant, about 1 minute.
3. Add fresh spinach to the skillet and cook until wilted, stirring occasionally.
4. Pour in heavy cream, stirring to combine with the spinach.
5. Cook for another 5 minutes until the cream has thickened slightly.
6. Season with salt, pepper, and a pinch of grated nutmeg, if desired.
7. Remove from heat and serve hot as a creamy and indulgent side dish.
   Nutritional Info (per serving): Calories: 250 | Fat: 23g | Carbs: 8g | Protein: 5g
   Student Vegetarian Function: Creamed spinach is a rich and comforting side dish that pairs well with roasted vegetables, grilled tofu, or pasta dishes.

CREAMED CORN

Prep: 5 mins | Cook: 10 mins | Serves: 4

INGREDIENTS:

- 4 cups frozen or canned corn kernels (US & UK)
- 1/4 cup butter (US & UK)
- 1/4 cup heavy cream (US) / double cream (UK)
- Salt and pepper, to taste
- Optional: chopped fresh herbs (parsley, chives), grated Parmesan cheese

INSTRUCTIONS:

1. In a skillet, melt butter over medium heat.
2. Add corn kernels to the skillet and cook until heated through.
3. Pour in heavy cream, stirring to combine with the corn.
4. Cook for another 5 minutes until the cream has thickened slightly.
5. Season with salt, pepper, and chopped fresh herbs, if desired.
6. Optional: Stir in grated Parmesan cheese for added flavor.
7. Remove from heat and serve hot as a comforting and creamy side dish.
   Nutritional Info (per serving): Calories: 250 | Fat: 17g | Carbs: 24g | Protein: 4g
   Student Vegetarian Function: Creamed corn is a classic and comforting side dish that pairs well with grilled vegetables, tofu, or vegetarian roasts.

MAC AND CHEESE BITES

Prep: 15 mins | Cook: 15 mins | Serves: 4

INGREDIENTS:

- 2 cups cooked macaroni pasta (US & UK)

- 1 cup shredded cheddar cheese (US & UK)
- 1/2 cup milk (US & UK)
- 1/4 cup grated Parmesan cheese (US & UK)
- 1 egg, beaten (US & UK)
- Salt and pepper, to taste
- Optional: breadcrumbs, chopped fresh herbs (parsley, chives)

INSTRUCTIONS:

1. Preheat the oven to 375°F (190°C) and grease a mini muffin tin.
2. In a bowl, mix together cooked macaroni, shredded cheddar cheese, milk, grated Parmesan cheese, beaten egg, salt, and pepper.
3. Spoon the mac and cheese mixture into the prepared mini muffin tin, filling each cup.
4. Optional: Sprinkle breadcrumbs over the tops of the mac and cheese bites for a crispy crust.
5. Bake for 12-15 minutes until the edges are golden and crispy.
6. Remove from the oven and let cool slightly before removing from the muffin tin.
7. Serve mac and cheese bites as a fun and portable side dish or snack.
   Nutritional Info (per serving): Calories: 300 | Fat: 15g | Carbs: 28g | Protein: 14g
   Student Vegetarian Function: Mac and cheese bites are a playful twist on the classic comfort food, perfect for parties, potlucks, or casual dinners.

LENTIL MEATLOAF

Prep: 15 mins | Cook: 45 mins | Serves: 4

INGREDIENTS:

- 1 cup cooked lentils (US & UK)
- 1 onion, finely chopped (US & UK)
- 2 cloves garlic, minced (US & UK)
- 1 carrot, grated (US & UK)
- 1 celery stalk, finely chopped (US & UK)
- 1/2 cup breadcrumbs (US & UK)
- 1/4 cup ketchup (US & UK)
- 1 tablespoon soy sauce (US & UK)
- 1 teaspoon dried thyme (US & UK)
- Salt and pepper, to taste

INSTRUCTIONS:

1. Preheat the oven to 375°F (190°C) and grease a loaf pan.
2. In a bowl, mix together cooked lentils, chopped onion, minced garlic, grated carrot, chopped celery, breadcrumbs, ketchup, soy sauce, dried thyme, salt, and pepper.
3. Transfer the lentil mixture to the greased loaf pan, pressing down to form a loaf shape.
4. Bake for 40-45 minutes until the lentil meatloaf is firm and golden on top.
5. Remove from the oven and let rest for a few minutes before slicing.
6. Serve lentil meatloaf with mashed potatoes and roasted vegetables.
   Nutritional Info (per serving): Calories: 280 | Fat: 4g | Carbs: 50g | Protein: 13g

Student Vegetarian Function: Lentil meatloaf is a hearty and protein-packed alternative to traditional meatloaf, perfect for a satisfying vegetarian dinner.

CAULIFLOWER STEAK

Prep: 10 mins | Cook: 20 mins | Serves: 2

INGREDIENTS:

- 1 large cauliflower head (US & UK)
- 2 tablespoons olive oil (US & UK)
- 1 teaspoon smoked paprika (US & UK)
- Salt and pepper, to taste
- Optional: garlic powder, lemon wedges, fresh herbs (parsley, thyme)

INSTRUCTIONS:

1. Preheat the oven to 400°F (200°C) and line a baking sheet with parchment paper.
2. Trim the cauliflower head and slice it into thick "steaks" about 1-inch thick.
3. In a bowl, mix together olive oil, smoked paprika, salt, pepper, and any additional seasonings.
4. Brush both sides of each cauliflower steak with the oil mixture.
5. Place the cauliflower steaks on the prepared baking sheet.
6. Roast in the oven for 15-20 minutes, flipping halfway through, until cauliflower is golden and tender.
7. Remove from the oven and serve hot with lemon wedges and fresh herbs, if desired.
   Nutritional Info (per serving): Calories: 150 | Fat: 10g | Carbs: 14g | Protein: 5g
   Student Vegetarian Function: Cauliflower steaks are a flavorful and satisfying vegetarian main course or side dish that's easy to prepare and packed with nutrients.

MUSHROOM WELLINGTON

Prep: 20 mins | Cook: 30 mins | Serves: 4

INGREDIENTS:

- 1 sheet puff pastry, thawed (US & UK)
- 2 cups mixed mushrooms, finely chopped (US & UK)
- 1 onion, finely chopped (US & UK)
- 2 cloves garlic, minced (US & UK)
- 1 tablespoon olive oil (US & UK)
- 2 tablespoons chopped fresh herbs (thyme, rosemary, parsley) (US & UK)
- Salt and pepper, to taste
- 1/4 cup breadcrumbs (US & UK)
- 1/4 cup grated Parmesan cheese (US & UK)
- 1 egg, beaten (for egg wash) (US & UK)

INSTRUCTIONS:

1. Preheat the oven to 400°F (200°C) and line a baking sheet with parchment paper.
2. In a skillet, heat olive oil over medium heat. Add chopped onion and garlic, sauté until softened.

3. Add chopped mushrooms and cook until they release their moisture and start to brown.
4. Stir in fresh herbs, salt, and pepper. Remove from heat and let cool slightly.
5. Roll out the puff pastry sheet on a lightly floured surface into a rectangle.
6. Spread the mushroom mixture evenly over the pastry sheet, leaving a border around the edges.
7. Sprinkle breadcrumbs and grated Parmesan cheese over the mushroom mixture.
8. Roll up the puff pastry tightly, sealing the edges with a bit of water. Place seam side down on the prepared baking sheet.
9. Brush the top and sides of the pastry with beaten egg for a golden finish.
10. Bake in the preheated oven for 25-30 minutes until the pastry is golden and crisp.
11. Remove from the oven and let rest for a few minutes before slicing.
12. Serve mushroom Wellington slices with a side salad or roasted vegetables.
    Nutritional Info (per serving): Calories: 350 | Fat: 22g | Carbs: 30g | Protein: 8g
    Student Vegetarian Function: Mushroom Wellington is an elegant and impressive dish that's perfect for special occasions or dinner parties, showcasing the versatility of mushrooms as a meat substitute.

NUT LOAF

Prep: 15 mins | Cook: 1 hour | Serves: 6

INGREDIENTS:

- 1 cup mixed nuts (walnuts, almonds, cashews), chopped (US & UK)
- 1 cup breadcrumbs (US & UK)
- 1 onion, finely chopped (US & UK)
- 2 cloves garlic, minced (US & UK)
- 1 carrot, grated (US & UK)
- 1 celery stalk, finely chopped (US & UK)
- 1 tablespoon olive oil (US & UK)
- 2 tablespoons tomato paste (US & UK)
- 2 tablespoons soy sauce (US & UK)
- 1 tablespoon Worcestershire sauce (US & UK)
- 1/2 cup vegetable broth (US & UK)
- Salt and pepper, to taste

INSTRUCTIONS:

1. Preheat the oven to 350°F (175°C) and grease a loaf pan.
2. In a skillet, heat olive oil over medium heat. Add chopped onion, minced garlic, grated carrot, and chopped celery. Sauté until softened.
3. Stir in tomato paste, soy sauce, Worcestershire sauce, and vegetable broth. Cook for a few minutes until well combined.
4. In a large bowl, combine chopped nuts, breadcrumbs, and the sautéed vegetable mixture. Mix well.
5. Season with salt and pepper to taste.
6. Transfer the nut mixture into the greased loaf pan, pressing down firmly.
7. Bake in the preheated oven for 50-60 minutes until the nut loaf is firm and golden on top.
8. Remove from the oven and let cool for a few minutes before slicing.
9. Serve nut loaf slices with mashed potatoes and steamed vegetables.

Nutritional Info (per serving): Calories: 300 | Fat: 20g | Carbs: 25g | Protein: 10g

Student Vegetarian Function: Nut loaf is a hearty and satisfying vegetarian alternative to traditional meatloaf, ideal for Sunday dinners or holiday meals.

ROOT VEGETABLE GRATIN

Prep: 20 mins | Cook: 45 mins | Serves: 6

INGREDIENTS:

- 2 large potatoes, peeled and thinly sliced (US & UK)
- 2 large sweet potatoes, peeled and thinly sliced (US & UK)
- 2 parsnips, peeled and thinly sliced (US & UK)
- 2 carrots, peeled and thinly sliced (US & UK)
- 1 onion, thinly sliced (US & UK)
- 2 cloves garlic, minced (US & UK)
- 1 cup heavy cream (US) / double cream (UK)
- 1 cup grated Gruyere cheese (US & UK)
- Salt and pepper, to taste
- Fresh thyme leaves, for garnish (optional)

INSTRUCTIONS:

1. Preheat the oven to 375°F (190°C) and grease a baking dish.
2. In a bowl, mix together sliced potatoes, sweet potatoes, parsnips, carrots, onion, and minced garlic.
3. Layer the mixed vegetables in the greased baking dish, alternating with grated Gruyere cheese.
4. Pour heavy cream evenly over the vegetable layers.
5. Season with salt and pepper to taste.
6. Cover the baking dish with foil and bake for 30 minutes.
7. Remove the foil and bake for an additional 15 minutes until the top is golden and bubbly.
8. Remove from the oven and let rest for a few minutes before serving.
9. Garnish with fresh thyme leaves, if desired.
10. Serve root vegetable gratin as a comforting and flavorful side dish.
    Nutritional Info (per serving): Calories: 350 | Fat: 22g | Carbs: 30g | Protein: 10g
    Student Vegetarian Function: Root vegetable gratin is a delicious and hearty dish that highlights the natural sweetness and earthy flavors of seasonal vegetables.

BUTTERNUT SQUASH RISOTTO

Prep: 10 mins | Cook: 30 mins | Serves: 4

INGREDIENTS:

- 1 small butternut squash, peeled, seeded, and diced (US & UK)
- 1 onion, finely chopped (US & UK)
- 2 cloves garlic, minced (US & UK)
- 1 cup Arborio rice (US & UK)
- 4 cups vegetable broth (US & UK)
- 1/2 cup dry white wine (optional) (US & UK)

- 1/2 cup grated Parmesan cheese (US & UK)
- 2 tablespoons butter (US & UK)
- Salt and pepper, to taste
- Fresh sage leaves, for garnish (optional)

INSTRUCTIONS:

1. In a large skillet or pot, heat olive oil over medium heat. Add chopped onion and minced garlic, sauté until softened.
2. Add diced butternut squash and Arborio rice to the skillet, stirring to coat in the oil
3. Pour in dry white wine (if using) and cook until the wine is absorbed.
4. Gradually add vegetable broth, one ladle at a time, stirring frequently and allowing the rice to absorb the liquid before adding more.
5. Continue cooking and adding broth until the rice is creamy and tender, about 20-25 minutes.
6. Stir in grated Parmesan cheese and butter, mixing until melted and incorporated.
7. Season with salt and pepper to taste.
8. Remove from heat and let rest for a few minutes before serving.
9. Garnish with fresh sage leaves, if desired.
10. Serve butternut squash risotto as a comforting and flavorful main course or side dish.
    Nutritional Info (per serving): Calories: 350 | Fat: 12g | Carbs: 50g | Protein: 8g
    Student Vegetarian Function: Butternut squash risotto is a creamy and satisfying dish that celebrates the flavors of fall, perfect for cozy dinners or special occasions.

CONCLUSION

Whether you're just getting started on your vegetarian journey or have been meat-free for years, this cookbook has hopefully inspired you with plenty of delicious, affordable and nutritious recipe ideas perfect for the student lifestyle. As you've seen, going vegetarian is far from boring or depriving! With a little creativity and effort, veggie-based meals can be just as flavorful and satisfying as their meat-centric counterparts. By now you should have all the tools, tips and recipes you need to easily prepare balanced vegetarian meals, no matter your skill level in the kitchen. You've got options for every meal, craving and occasion from wholesome breakfasts to energizing snacks, hearty mains to lightened-up treats. The best part? These dishes can all be made in basic kitchens with limited equipment and budget-friendly ingredients. Of course, this is just the beginning. As you continue your vegetarian journey, I encourage you to experiment, play with new ingredients and recipes, and discover what you like. Make substitutions where needed based on your personal tastes, dietary needs and what's available near campus. Get creative with combining flavors and trying new veggie varieties from the farmer's market or global food aisles. Gradually building up your culinary skills and recipe repertoire is all part of the fun! Don't forget that eating veggie for health is about so much more than just what you put on your plate. Nurture yourself in other ways to get plenty of rest, stay hydrated, find active hobbies you enjoy, spend time with loved ones. Caring for your whole self physically, mentally and socially is key to happily sustaining this lifestyle throughout your busy college days. Speaking of your social life, going vegetarian certainly doesn't have to mean missing out. This book arms you with tons of crowd pleasing, shareable veggie nosh like mezze platters, loaded nachos, baked veggie apps and sliceable pizzas. When dining out with friends or going to potlucks, scope out the veggie options beforehand and don't be afraid to ask about ingredient swaps or modifications to menu items. As for dating as a vegetarian, it's a great way to weed out incompatible interests right off the bat! But don't rule someone out simply because they're not veggie too just politely explain your reasons for not consuming meat if it comes up. You may find they're curious to learn more about this way of eating. Who knows, you may even inspire others to join you on this plant-based path. On that note, don't be afraid to lean into your vegetarian identity. Just as this lifestyle aligns with your personal values, it's an opportunity to advocate for causes you're passionate about like environmental conservation, combating world hunger, ethical treatment of animals and more. Look for ways to get involved with vegetarian and vegan clubs, meat-free cafes, community gardens, food assistance programs and other initiatives on campus. Join up with like-minded people to organize meatless Monday events in your dining hall or start a vegan baked goods business to raise money for a good cause. Above all, always be proud to make choices that positively impact the world around you at every meal and beyond. Though your reasons for going vegetarian may evolve over the years, you're still doing an amazing thing for your health, the planet and perhaps even your spiritual beliefs. Staying committed to this lifestyle while juggling a busy student schedule is no small feat and you should feel incredibly empowered by that! So, here's to an incredible, deliciously veggie-packed four years ahead. May this cookbook inspire you to get creative in the kitchen, nurture your overall wellbeing, embrace compassionate living and make the most of this incredibly vibrant time in your life. Wishing you success and happiness, one flavorful meat-free meal at a time!

Printed in Great Britain
by Amazon

50504874R00059